true stories from the edge

Andreas Schroeder

thieves!

Ten stories of surprising
heists, comical capers,
and daring escapades

ANNICK PRESS

TORONTO + NEW YORK + VANCOUVER

Annick Press Ltd.

We acknowledge the support of the Canada Council for the Arts, the Ontario Arts
Council, and the Government of Canada through the Book Publishing Industry
Development Program (BPIDP) for our publishing activities.

Edited by Pam Robertson
Copy-edited by Elizabeth McLean
Cover design and interior design by Irvin Cheung/iCheung Design
Cover illustration by Scott Cameron

Cataloging in Publication Data
Schroeder, Andreas, 1946–
Thieves! / written by Andreas Schroeder.

(True stories from the edge)
Includes bibliographical references and index.
ISBN 1-55037-933-X (bound).—ISBN 1-55037-932-1 (pbk.)

1. Robbery—Juvenile literature. 2. Theft—Juvenile literature.
3. Thieves—Juvenile literature. I. Title. II. Series.

HV6652.S36 2005   j364.15'52   C2005-901152-1

The text was typeset in Bembo

Published in the U.S.A. by	**Distributed in Canada by**	**Distributed in the U.S.A. by**
Annick Press (U.S.) Ltd.	Firefly Books Ltd.	Firefly Books (U.S.) Inc.
	66 Leek Crescent	P.O. Box 1338
	Richmond Hill, ON	Ellicott Station
	L4B 1H1	Buffalo, NY 14205

Printed and bound in Canada

Visit us at **www.annickpress.com**

Contents

Look for more exciting titles in the award-winning series *True Stories from the Edge:*

Tunnels! by Diane Swanson

People have been tunneling since the Stone Age. These gripping stories of human drama beneath the ground are fast-paced and tension-filled.

Escapes! by Laura Scandiffio

History is full of daring escapes. The exhilarating stories in this collection take readers around the world and across the ages.

Scams! by Andreas Schroeder

Scam artists have been tricking people for a very long time. These dramatic stories explore some of the most outrageous and inventive swindlers of all time.

Fires! by Tanya Lloyd Kyi

Step into the blinding flames, the choking smoke, and the waves of heat that brought humans face-to-face with one of the world's mightiest natural forces.

Acknowledgments

I would like to express my profound gratitude to my editor
Pam Robertson, whose cheerful assistance proved invaluable
too many times to count. Thanks also to Elizabeth McLean, for
alert copy-editing that saved me more than once from certain
embarrassment.

Introduction

Trying for the Big Score

OF ALL THE KINDS OF CRIMES that human beings have committed, stealing is probably the most common. Almost everyone has stolen something at some point in their lives. The impulse to simply take something we want—even if it belongs to someone else—can be irresistible.

It usually starts small—a boy palms a candy bar at a corner grocery store; a girl pockets a bottle of perfume at a drugstore. They get away with it once or twice, and then they're caught. Usually the embarrassment and shame of being caught is enough to put a permanent stop to a budding thief.

But not always. Cassie Chadwick, who became one of North America's most notorious female embezzlers, stole from an early age: jewelry, cosmetics, clothes, even groceries. She was often caught, but it never slowed her down. She stole so much and so often, a judge eventually pronounced her insane. He underestimated her. In 1902, she asked a group of Cleveland bankers to lend her huge sums of money based on her claim that she would be inheriting part of the estate of America's richest industrialist, Andrew Carnegie. She "proved" this by taking the banks' lawyers by carriage to Carnegie's mansion in New York, and asking them to wait (she said Carnegie didn't like lawyers) while she met with Carnegie.

She was inside for nearly half an hour. When she came out, she triumphantly showed them two checks for almost a million dollars, made out to Cassie Chadwick and signed by Carnegie.

The lawyers were impressed, and Cassie got her loans—which, of course, she never repaid. To pull off this scam, she had simply knocked on the door, told the maid she was feeling faint, and asked for permission to lie down on a bench in the foyer for a few moments. The kind-hearted maid had agreed. After half an hour, Cassie had "felt better" and left the house. The lawyers had assumed she'd been spending all this time with Andrew Carnegie—who, it turned out, hadn't even been home.

STEALING, OF COURSE, becomes easier if your victims seem to beg you to do it—by leaving their front door unlocked, or their keys dangling in the ignition. That, in effect, was what the French government did in the 1960s, when it decided to pay its citizens to have more babies, to offset that country's alarmingly low birthrate. It offered French families annual payments of $1,100 each for their first two kids, $1,500 for their third, and $1,850 for every fourth and additional child.

This offer quickly attracted the attention of a Romany gypsy named Jimenez Moreno. Moreno already had a family of 12, so he stood to benefit rather handsomely from the government's plan. But he soon realized there was even greater booty to be had. Since the plan didn't require a fixed address, he loaded his family into a big camper van, hit the road, and, using a variety of names, registered his family for the baby bonus in every town through which he passed. He did this without let-up for five whole years. By the time the government realized what was going on, Moreno's family had been registered in 354 towns, and he had stolen almost $15 million from the plan. And the French government never retrieved a penny of that money. Someone warned Moreno that the police had discovered his deception, and he quickly disappeared over the border into Spain. He was never caught.

Thieves like Moreno, however, are the exception. Most thieves are eventually caught—even the really successful ones. And when they're caught, they generally find themselves in a serious fix. That's because most thieves steal in hopes that they'll make the big score one day, the theft that will allow them to retire to some South Seas island with truckloads of money. But thieves are also notorious spendthrifts. When they make a big score, they party. They feel a great need to show off their success—and blowing their ill-gotten gains on extravagant parties is one way to do this. Another is to buy huge mansions, flashy cars, or luxury yachts. The problem is that to spend a lot of money, you've got to keep stealing a lot of money. So a thief's life can become a treadmill—and when the police finally come knocking, that treadmill crashes. Any money left is usually taken by the lawyers and the courts, and if the thief is sentenced to jail time, his possessions on the outside are often stolen by former partners or friends.

Many professional thieves end their careers broke and disillusioned.

SOAPY SMITH IS A GOOD EXAMPLE. At the height of his thieving career, in the 1890s, Soapy Smith practically owned the town of Skagway, Alaska, which was the doorway to the Alaska gold rush. After years of thieving solo in the American Midwest, Soapy had gone north and become so successful that he now had a whole army of thieves working for him. They were a well-organized crew. Every boat that arrived in Skagway was met by a "town official" who informed all the passengers that a decent haircut was a legal sanitary requirement in Skagway. As the passengers sat in their barber chairs, the barbers (who were also on Soapy's payroll) grilled them for information, determining who had money, who was an easy victim, and who was too well-connected or too politically powerful to rob. Anyone deemed a good candidate had a faint "V" cut into the hair at the back of his head. Such easily recognized people were invariably robbed the same day by Soapy or one of his roving thieves.

It was such an effective racket that by the 1890s it was estimated that over a quarter of the roughly $2 billion worth of gold that was hauled out of the mining claims in Alaska each year passed through Soapy Smith's hands. And yet when Soapy Smith died from an assassin's bullet in 1898, it turned out he had precisely $85 to his name. That was all there was. It wasn't even enough money for a tombstone. The citizens of Skagway simply scratched Soapy's name on an old piece of board and hammered it into the ground above his grave.

JOE WEIL, NICKNAMED "THE YELLOW KID" after a popular comic strip character of the time, was determined to beat the odds and he almost did. As one of America's most famous thieves in the 1920s and 30s, he always wore the most expensive clothes, smoked the most expensive cigars, and drove the flashiest cars. He specialized in the rackets—fleecing his victims with fixed card games, fixed horse races, and phony stocks and bonds. But Weil's wife was devoutly religious, and kept trying to talk her husband into quitting his life of crime. Finally, at age 50, Weil could see that his thieving days were becoming numbered, so he agreed. He stopped stealing and invested his ill-gotten gains in a legitimate hotel. His wife was enormously relieved.

But the joke was on Weil—*and* his wife. As soon as Weil's friends heard about his hotel, they all showed up at his door.

They made the place their favorite hangout. It became so noto-rious for its crooked clientele that law-abiding people stopped patronizing the place. Meanwhile, Weil's friends weren't paying their bills.

"Your thieving friends are stealing you blind!" his wife com-plained, and it was true. Weil's hotel soon went broke, and so did Weil. He wound up living off his wife's store-clerk salary.

BILLY MINER ("THE GREY FOX"), the last of the famous American train robbers that included the likes of Butch Cassidy, The Sundance Kid, and Jesse James, might have made the big score and lived happily ever after, because Billy didn't believe in partying. He was quiet, modest, and avoided flashy clothes or luxurious possessions—or anything else that might make him stand out in a crowd. But Billy had an unusual prob-lem: he simply couldn't stop being polite. His mother had trained him well—too well, as it turned out—and this marked him as effectively as those V's in the hair of Soapy Smith's victims. No matter how much he tried to disguise himself for his robberies, the train passengers invariably noticed how polite he was, and that's the first thing they told the police. "He kept saying please and thank you, and he was so gentlemanly."

The police immediately knew exactly who they were talking about, and Miner's picture would once again adorn the walls of US Postal offices all over America. Billy Miner died penniless in a prison in Georgia in 1913.

OCCASIONALLY A THIEF has gone on to become a folk hero. The English highwayman Robin Hood was undeniably a robber, but because he shared some of his loot with the poor, he became a symbol of the struggle between the privileged rich and the downtrodden poor of England. Over time, his story became more legend than fact. The Australian outlaw Ned Kelly belongs in the same category. He was a horse and cattle thief, which would ordinarily have put him in the lowest ranks of Australian society. But in Australia in the mid-19th century, a struggle had developed between rich landowners and small farmers. The farmers bitterly resented the way the landowners had used their political connections to take possession of all the best land. As the son of a small farmer, Ned Kelly saw nothing wrong with "rescuing" the odd cow or horse from landowners who, in his view, had themselves stolen half the surrounding countryside. The landowners, needless to say, saw it differently. They decided to make an example of Ned Kelly.

Under pressure from the landowners, the police hounded Ned and his family relentlessly. They were arrested and jailed again and again, often on trumped-up charges. Finally, Ned Kelly had had enough. He and several friends surprised half a dozen police officers who were hunting for them in the Wombat Range mountains, and shot three of the constables dead.

From that point on, the Kelly gang was on the run. Over the next two years, they roamed the countryside, robbing banks for pocket money and evading one police ambush after another. Finally, in 1880, an informer betrayed them in the town of Glenrowan.

That's where the gang made its last stand, wearing suits of iron armor they had made themselves. It didn't save them. Dozens of police constables opened fire, and three of the gang were killed. Ned Kelly was wounded and captured. He was tried, sentenced, and hanged in the Old Melbourne Gaol, becoming an almost instant Australian legend. He became a symbol for courage, recklessness, and the refusal to be pushed around by corrupt officialdom. More books, films, plays, and documentaries have been produced about Ned Kelly than any other figure in Australian history, and his fame continues to grow to this day.

MOST THIEVES STEAL MONEY, or its equivalent: valuables that can be pawned for money, or valuables that would have cost them money. But there are exceptions. In doing the research for this book, I came across the astonishing story of Charles-Hippolyte Delperch de la Bussière, a Parisian actor during the French Revolution. It was 1793, King Louis XVI had just been assassinated, and a revolutionary by the name of Robespierre had seized control of France. As head of a group called "The Committee of Public Safety," Robespierre was now busily arresting and chopping the heads off as many French aristocrats as he could lay his hands on. Charles-Hippolyte (let's call him Charlie) would have preferred to keep making his living as an actor, but Robespierre had shut down all the theaters. So Charlie applied for a job at the Committee of Public Safety. It had such an innocent-sounding name after all. But once he got a job there as a filing clerk, he quickly realized what the Committee was *really* doing.

Charlie's job looked innocent, too. People brought files to his desk, and all he had to do was make certain all the documentation was there and that it was arranged in the correct order. Then he was supposed to send the files down to a department called The Revolutionary Tribunal. But what Charlie soon discovered was that once those files had been sent to the Tribunal, the people listed in them were as good as dead. The Tribunal was supposed to be a legal court, but nobody was ever found "not guilty." Every person whose file Charlie organized was doomed to have his or her head chopped off.

At first, Charlie tried to ignore this fact. The people whose files he was organizing were rich aristocrats, and Charlie had never much liked aristocrats. Most of the ones he knew were snobbish, arrogant, and greedy. But soon it wasn't just aristocrats. It was teachers, doctors, students. And then artists. Writers. *Actors*. Charlie began to recognize some of the names on the files coming across his desk.

On the day he began to organize the file of a fellow actor from the Theatre Française where Charlie had performed, Charlie realized he couldn't do this anymore. He was condemning his own friends to death. True, he hadn't actually made these decisions, but by sending down the files he was making them happen. On the other hand, it began to dawn on him that he might be in a far more influential position than he'd realized. Because if he *didn't* send down a file, what then?

He shoved his friend's file to the bottom of the pile, and kept it there for a week.

Nothing happened. Nobody from the Tribunal asked about that file. Nobody from the Committee did, either. Charlie realized that there was no other connection between the two agencies. He was it.

By this time, files of other friends were landing on his desk. The director of a play he'd been in several years ago. A producer who'd given him a break. More fellow actors. The piles on his desk were getting higher.

Charlie considered his options. He couldn't just shove the files down his shirt and take them home, because everyone was searched coming and going at the building's front door. He couldn't throw them into the garbage, because all garbage bins and wastebaskets were regularly checked. The windows were painted closed, so that wasn't an option. What to do?

Charlie was eating his lunch when the answer suddenly struck him. He looked around—nobody was watching. He casually picked up a piece of paper from one of his friends' files and—ate it.

It tasted pretty awful, but a big glug of water helped it down. That's when Charlie realized what he had to do.

Over the next 18 months, Charlie stole and ate about 15 files per week—roughly 3 files a day. He munched on documents all day long. He took entire files with him to the bathroom and choked them down. His tongue tasted like rotten leather and the inside of his mouth broke out in a nasty rash, but he kept it up. By the time he was finally caught, he'd eaten the files of 1,153 condemned countrymen. Every one of them was saved.

Charlie was charged with stealing government documents. He didn't deny it. His case was heard by the Tribunal, and he was sentenced to have his head chopped off. Fortunately, Napoleon overthrew Robespierre's regime less than a week later, and Charlie (along with thousands of other condemned prisoners) was set free. He was celebrated as a hero, but he didn't live long to enjoy his fame. He died soon after from the effects of the toxic substances in all the ink and paper he had eaten.

Most thieves are crooks, it's true. They cause everyone a great deal of grief and misery.

But now and then there are thieves like Charles-Hippolyte Delperch de la Bussière who steal just to help others.

THE 10 STORIES THAT FOLLOW are taken from a wide variety of documented sources. They all happened within the past 150 years, and most of them involve professional thieves who spent their lives figuring out ingenious ways to steal other people's possessions.

The thieves portrayed in these stories were all serious criminals, but some were more talented than others. As a result, some of the stories are perhaps funnier than their perpetrators intended. Some are heart-warming, and some are heart-breaking. Every one of them would make a fantastic movie—at least four of them already have. And all of them share one common characteristic: they make for great reading.

On the Run
with Mona Lisa

THE THREE ITALIAN WORKMEN who joined the crowds swarming eagerly through the vast Musée du Louvre in Paris on the Sunday afternoon of August 20, 1911, were trying very hard to look like tourists.

The man in the lead, Vincenzo Perugia, was a short, stocky cabinetmaker who wore a dark suit and a straw hat. His two companions, the Lancelotti brothers, were wearing their Sunday jackets and trousers. One of the Lancelottis carried a folding camera over his shoulder.

The Louvre, France's most renowned art museum, was a popular tourist attraction. Its more than 200 luxurious, high-ceilinged galleries contained thousands of the world's most famous and valuable paintings.

The three men sauntered through gallery after gallery, casually following the crowds. Here and there, they paused, pretending to study the magnificent paintings. From time to time, they glanced at their watches.

At 3:45 p.m., Perugia turned and headed for a small gallery named the Salle Duchâtel. There, he stopped before a large Bramantino hanging on the gallery's east wall. The Lancelotti brothers joined him, and the three men fell into a deep contemplation of the masterpiece.

A guard stuck his head through the gallery entrance. "*On ferme!*" he called. It was almost closing time. He left and they could hear his voice in the next gallery. "*On ferme! On ferme, mesdames et messieurs!*"

People began drifting out of the room. The three men didn't move. Finally, the last couple left.

"Now!" Perugia hissed. He reached behind the Bramantino and pushed on a hidden spring in the wall. A narrow door opened inward behind the painting, revealing a small storeroom. The three men slipped inside and closed the door.

Outside they could still hear the faint voices of the guards making their rounds, herding the last remaining tourists toward the front door. "*On ferme, mesdames et messieurs! On ferme!*"

THE NEXT MORNING, the three men awoke to the sound of shuffling footsteps and the clatter of a cleaner's cart outside the storeroom door. On Mondays, the Louvre was closed to the public for maintenance and repairs. Instead of tourists, an army of cleaners, electricians, plumbers, carpenters, and plasterers swarmed through the museum. They were all dressed in loose, white, museum-issue smocks, which served as both uniform and identity card. Anyone wearing such a smock on Mondays at the Louvre was obviously a museum employee.

Perugia and his accomplices got up, drew identical white smocks from under their jackets and pulled them on over their street clothes. Now they were part of the Louvre's maintenance crew. They waited until the steps had faded away and then opened the door a crack. They were in luck—the gallery was empty. The brothers quickly picked up a broom and a mop they found leaning against one of the walls. Perugia pulled a dusting cloth out of his pocket. They now proceeded to sweep and mop and dust their way from room to room, heading steadily toward the gallery that contained the painting they had been hired to steal.

The gallery was the Salle Carré, and the painting was Leonardo da Vinci's *Mona Lisa*.

It was the most famous portrait in the world.

Vincenzo Perugia knew exactly where the *Mona Lisa* was hanging, and not just because he had seen her in the Salle Carré the day before. Several years ago, Perugia had been employed by the Louvre to build vandal-resistant glass coverings for some of the museum's most valuable paintings. He had taken the job because he'd been desperate for work, but the assignment had appalled him. Imagine! Imprisoning the *Mona Lisa* in a cage! These crazy Frenchmen simply had no appreciation for art! Especially Italian art, like the *Mona Lisa*. They didn't deserve her, that was his opinion. Hadn't he read somewhere that she'd actually been stolen and brought to France by Napoleon? It wouldn't have surprised him a bit. Ever since he'd come to France, he'd been treated like dirt and paid barely enough to live on.

One of the Lancelotti brothers cleared his throat meaningfully behind him. Perugia looked up and realized that with all his brooding and grumbling, he hadn't realized that they'd reached the Salle Carré.

And there she was. The *Mona Lisa*. Hanging serenely between Correggio's *Mystic Marriage* on her left, and Titian's *Allegory* on her right. Winking mischievously at him, he was sure of it. Ah, what a woman! It was enough to make a man homesick.

And then, Vincenzo Perugia and the Lancelotti brothers simply did what maintenance workers were doing all over the Louvre that morning—taking down paintings for rearranging, repair, restoration, or reframing. No one challenged their actions. No one demanded an explanation. They simply lifted the world's most famous portrait from the wall and carried it out of the Salle

Carré, through the Grande Galerie, across the Salle des Sept Metres, and out through a doorway into a service stairway.

Once they'd closed the door behind them, however, their suppressed excitement burst to the surface. Bounding down the stairs to the ground floor with the portrait clutched in his arms, Perugia scuttled behind the staircase and began slashing frantically at the heavy tape that held it in its vandal-proof frame. While one of the brothers began taking apart the frame with a small crowbar, the other went to work on the outside door with a duplicate key.

"*Mannagia*! This stupid key won't work!"

"Wiggle it and twist it around," Perugia advised, without looking up.

More rattling and jiggling. "It won't turn!"

Perugia handed off the portrait and tried the key. It slid into the lock easily, but refused to turn. No amount of struggling budged it.

Alarmed, Perugia whipped out a screwdriver and began to take apart the lock. His hands trembled, and the screwdriver kept slipping off the screws. Finally the doorknob fell off and the face plate came loose.

"*Attenti!*" one of the Lancelotti brothers hissed. "Somebody's coming!"

The other brother lunged behind the stairs with the portrait.

The door above them opened and a workman carrying a plumber's toolkit came down the stairs. Halfway down, he noticed two annoyed-looking maintenance men standing at the outside door below.

"This stupid doorknob has fallen off and now we can't get out!" one of them shouted in disgust. "Everything in this place is falling apart! They should just tear everything down and start over!"

"*Du calme*," the plumber replied soothingly. "*Du calme, messieurs.*" These excitable Italians—always making everything into an opera. He pulled out his own key, slid it into the lock, turned it, and then used a pair of pliers to substitute for the missing doorknob. "There you go, *messieurs*. I'll put it on the maintenance report for tomorrow. But for now, better leave the door ajar. Someone else might have the same problem."

He waved and went cheerfully on his way.

Two minutes later, the *Mona Lisa* was in a cab with three very excited Italians, heading for Perugia's apartment a few city blocks away.

AMAZINGLY, it was a full 27 hours before the authorities at the Louvre realized the *Mona Lisa* was missing.

Even then, they hoped it was just a mistake. Had someone taken her to the Reproduction Shop to be photographed? Had she been sent down to the Restoration Shop for cleaning? Was she simply "in transit" between different shops? In an institution as vast as the Louvre, there was plenty of room for things to be misplaced.

But by Wednesday, August 23, every corner of the Louvre had been examined several times over, and the disassembled frame had been discovered in the stairwell. There was no longer any doubt about it—the most famous portrait in the world, and France's most beloved cultural treasure, had been stolen.

At that point, all hell broke loose.

"*UNIMAGINABLE!*" was the one-word headline of the Paris newspaper *Le Matin*.

"*INEXPLICABLE!*" echoed other French morning newspapers. "*INCROYABLE!*"

"*What audacious criminal, what mystifier, what manic collector, what insane lover, has committed this abduction?"* demanded the editors of the magazine *L'Illustration*.

Within hours, orders were telegraphed from the highest levels of government, sealing France's borders. Its harbors were closed and its railway stations were shut down. All outgoing trains, ships, and carriages were searched.

Police swarmed into the Louvre. Investigations were launched. Disciplinary hearings and reprimands multiplied. Heads rolled. The senior curator of the Louvre was fired. The Undersecretary for Fine Arts was forced to resign.

Given the facts of the case, it was decided that the theft must have been an inside job. The Louvre was ordered to produce a list of all persons who were or had been employees of the museum during the past five years. All persons on that list were to be interrogated by the police. Anyone with a police record was to be questioned especially thoroughly.

The Lancelotti brothers had never worked for the Louvre and had no police records. Perugia, however, qualified on both counts. He had worked for the Louvre and had twice been arrested—once on a charge of attempted robbery, once for the illegal possession of a knife. So he had reason to worry.

That reason increased when the police discovered a left thumbprint on the discarded frame in the stairwell.

But for some inexplicable reason, Perugia's police file turned out to contain only his *right* thumbprint—and opposing thumbprints are not identical. Plus, his employment record at the Louvre had been misfiled.

When the Louvre discovered this misfile three months later, the police finally did show up at Perugia's door. But after a two-hour interrogation, the officer saw no reason to arrest him—even though the officer's interrogation notes acknowledged that "according to information received, it appears that on 21 August last [i.e. the date of the theft], this man, who is normally at work at 7:00 a.m., did not arrive until 9:00 a.m.—an absence of two hours for which we have no explanation." Since authorities knew the *Mona Lisa* had been stolen on either Monday or Tuesday, one might have thought that such an observation would have set off alarm bells at the Préfecture de Police.

It didn't. Perugia's name was checked off the list, and the investigation moved on.

What the interrogating police officer hadn't realized was that during that entire interview *he had been sitting less than an arm's length away from the Mona Lisa!* Perugia had wrapped her in a linen cloth and hidden her in the false bottom he'd built into a wooden trunk.

And that's where she remained for the next two years, while La Sûreté Nationale de France continued its increasingly desperate search for her, and Vincenzo Perugia became more and more confused and angry.

The problem was, Perugia understood amazingly little about this robbery.

Earlier that summer, an elegantly dressed gentleman had called at Perugia's rooming house and explained that he wished to hire Perugia for an undertaking that, if successful, would earn him enough money to take care of him for many years to come. He seemed to know all about the Italian carpenter, his employment at the Louvre, his police record, and his growing bitterness toward the French.

The man proposed that Perugia steal the *Mona Lisa*—and he had the plan all worked out.

It was the Signore (as Perugia called him—the man had been careful never to disclose his name) who had gotten him the smocks, the duplicate key, the location of the hidden storeroom. He had spread a blueprint of the Louvre on Perugia's bed, showing him exactly where he would begin, where he would carry the painting, and how he would get it out. All Perugia had to do was arrange for the help of the Lancelotti brothers and steal the portrait.

For this, the Signore had agreed to pay Perugia a sum equivalent to about five years' income as a first installment—with the promise of a second installment in the same amount when "everything succeeded." (The Lancelotti brothers, he said, would only receive a first installment.) And the Signore had indeed paid everyone as agreed, on the day after the theft, when Perugia had met him to hand over the portrait. But to Perugia's astonishment, the Signore hadn't taken the portrait away. He'd merely admired it for a short while, then rewrapped it in its linen cloth and instructed Perugia to keep it hidden in his apartment "until it was required."

Perugia had assumed the Signore intended to ransom the portrait, selling it back to the Louvre for a hefty sum. But as the months passed by, there was no sign that any negotiations were taking place. The newspapers continued to deplore the loss of France's most beloved national treasure. The police kept up their relentless dragnet efforts to find the painting. And the Louvre—well, the Louvre had rather cleverly managed to turn its disaster into quite an advantage. More people were now visiting the museum to see the place where the famous portrait *wasn't,* than had ever come to see it when it *was.* Even two years after her disappearance, people were still laying so many flowers and wreaths beneath the *Mona Lisa*'s empty wall space in the Salle Carré that they had to be cleared away twice a day.

Meanwhile, Vincenzo Perugia was broke once again, and

still waiting for his second instalment. He was also getting the distinct impression that he had somehow been made a fool.

Finally, an idea occurred to him—an idea that seemed to address all of his feelings about how he had been treated in this country.

He would take the *Mona Lisa* home to Italy. That's what he would do. He would "repatriate" her. The French didn't deserve her. Only Italians could fully appreciate her. She belonged among her own kind, her own people, in a splendid art gallery in Milan, or maybe Florence. He had recently come across an ad in a Florence newspaper: *Artworks of all kinds purchased for good prices.* He would reply to that ad. He suspected that, unlike the stingy French, the Italians would probably pay a very good price for the *Mona Lisa.*

WHEN ALFREDO GERI, the gallery owner who had placed the ad in the Florence newspaper, received Vincenzo Perugia's letter, he was sure that this had to be a joke. He showed the letter to a few of his friends, who all agreed. But something eventually changed Geri's mind. He knew that the French police had recently acknowledged that they had completely run out of clues. He also knew that several French organizations had posted enormous rewards for the return of the portrait.

What could he lose? A few *lire* for a postage stamp.

One month, two letters, and three telegrams later, Alfredo Geri and Giovanni Poggi, director of Florence's world-famous Uffizi Gallery, stared in amazement as Perugia unwrapped the *Mona Lisa* and casually dropped her onto his unmade bed in a smelly little hotel room in Florence.

"My god," Geri breathed. "It's really her."

"Of course," Perugia shrugged. "What have I been telling you?"

Geri and Poggi examined the portrait wordlessly for some minutes. Then they looked at each other meaningfully. "Signore Perugia," Geri said carefully, "how much are you asking for this painting?"

Perugia shrugged again. "Five hundred thousand?" he suggested. It was an amount equivalent to about $100,000.

The two men smiled faintly. "We'll have the money for you by this afternoon," Geri said. "Please remain with the painting until then."

Perugia grinned happily. You see? Italians definitely appreciated art more than the French.

PERUGIA PROBABLY FELT A LITTLE DIFFERENTLY half an hour later when the Florence police—alerted by Geri and Poggi—hammered on his hotel room door and arrested him for the theft of the most famous portrait in the world. Perugia was outraged! He protested that they were making a big mistake. He hadn't stolen the *Mona Lisa*—he had merely rescued her! *Mannagia*, what was the world coming to if the police couldn't tell the difference between theft and rescue anymore! The rightful owners of the *Mona Lisa* were the citizens of Italy, and he, Perugia, had finally restored her to them! Was this the thanks he got?

During his four months in a Florence jail cell, while he waited to make this pitch to a judge, Perugia had plenty of time to tell his story to the press—and each time the story got better. Yes, certainly, he was the one who had masterminded the *Mona Lisa's* daring rescue. Just he himself, alone, yes. And, by the way, at enormous risk to his person and his career! Oh, yes, those French police could be vicious! No, his motives had never been financial—he didn't care a fig about money. It was his love of

Italy and his outrage at the injustice of it all—the *Mona Lisa* languishing in France, far from home, and locked in a vandal-proof cage. Imagine! In France, people spit on their art! But in Italy, people appreciated art! They didn't have to worry about vandals in their galleries...

The French press didn't pay much attention to the excitable little carpenter. They were just happy to know that their national treasure was safe. But the Italian press loved Perugia. They ate up his stories. They cheered him on. They especially enjoyed the way this simple Italian carpenter had totally hoodwinked the formidable French police.

It wasn't long before Perugia became a national hero. Money was raised for his defense. Letters of support and congratulations arrived by the sackful. So many people sent flowers, wine, and food that Perugia soon had to be moved to a bigger cell.

The judge, when Perugia finally got his hearing, seemed to be the only person in Italy who had his doubts about Perugia. He suspected him of being a "storyteller" and sentenced him to a further year and 15 days in prison. But the resulting public uproar convinced an appeal judge to pay more attention to the public mood. This judge made himself enormously popular by setting Perugia free, and announcing that French efforts to have Perugia extradited to face charges in France would be denied. (The fact that France hadn't actually bothered to request Perugia's extradition wasn't mentioned.) Perugia left the court a free man, surrounded by enthusiastic well-wishers.

THE MONA LISA WAS RETURNED to France via a triumphant tour that stopped in almost every major city between Rome and Paris. Everywhere she was exhibited, people turned out by the tens of thousands. Security and riot police had to be brought in several times. In Paris, after many official ceremonies, she was resettled in the Louvre, where over 100,000 people came to see her in the first two days alone. Finally, when the excitement died down a little, she was moved to a new, more easily monitored location in the Salle des États, where she remains to this day.

No one besides Perugia was ever arrested and tried for the theft of the *Mona Lisa*. (The Lancelotti brothers, although mentioned in several French police reports, were apparently not considered important enough to charge.)

SO WHO WAS THE TRUE MASTERMIND of the *Mona Lisa* theft, and why did he never take possession of the priceless portrait?

It wasn't until half a century later that investigative journalist and history writer Seymour Reit discovered the answer—and the daring scam that lay at the heart of the famous theft.

The Signore, Reit discovered, was an Argentine-born Paris art dealer by the name of Eduardo de Valfierno. In January of 1910, Valfierno had read an article in a Paris newspaper about various security lapses at the Louvre—including the fact that on maintenance Mondays, the entire museum was guarded by fewer than a dozen guards. This put an idea into his head.

Valfierno specialized in selling forged or stolen artwork to dishonest buyers, so his first instinct was to consider stealing the *Mona Lisa* to sell to one of his customers. But on reflection, he came up with a far more ingenious and profitable plan—a plan that would allow him to sell the famous portrait not once, but many times. Six times, as it turned out.

What Valfierno did was contact a number of very rich but dishonest art collectors to offer them the possibility of buying the world's most famous portrait "should she become available" (wink wink). The price was considerable—the equivalent of roughly $5 million today. Yet Valfierno apparently had little trouble finding six willing buyers—five of them American, one Brazilian.

With orders in hand, he returned to Paris to consult with Yves Chaudron—perhaps the most talented art forger in the western world at that time. Valfierno and Chaudron had worked together before and they trusted each other. Chaudron eventually agreed to forge six extremely high-quality copies of the *Mona Lisa*—copies so excellent, they even duplicated the chemical composition of Leonardo da Vinci's 15th-century paints, and imitated his exact brush strokes. It was a job that took Chaudron well over a year.

When they were done, Valfierno shipped five of the fakes to a warehouse in New York, and the sixth to a bank vault in Rio de Janeiro.

After that, everything fell into place like a line of dominoes. The real *Mona Lisa* was stolen on August 21, 1911. The newspaper headlines announcing her theft exploded across the world two days later. Valfierno waited for a few more days to make sure all six of his customers had heard the news—then sent each man a discreet note informing him that his "purchase" was on its way. When each man received his fake *Mona Lisa* a week later, each naturally assumed it was the portrait that had been stolen from the Louvre. Every one of Valfierno's suckers happily paid up.

Once he had been paid, of course, Valfierno had no further use for the real *Mona Lisa*. It didn't matter to him whether she was found or not. Their acceptance of the fakes had made every one of his customers a criminal accessory to the real *Mona Lisa*'s theft, so none of them could risk going to the police to complain.

It might have been tidier to destroy the real portrait, or to send Perugia his second payment to keep him quiet, but for some reason Valfierno did neither. Perhaps he wanted the real *Mona Lisa* restored to the world once she had filled his bank account.

Valfierno retired to Morocco, where he died a rich and free man in 1931.

Chaudron retired to a quiet life on the outskirts of Paris.

And Perugia—well, Perugia never stopped complaining that he'd gotten a raw deal financially. But on the other hand, he was able to dine out on his story anywhere in Italy for the rest of his life.

IF THE NIGHT GUARD employed by the Monarch Bay
Shopping Mall in the prosperous California town of Laguna
Niguel had been doing his job, he might have noticed them:
four men in a 1962 Oldsmobile Super 88, slowly circling the
mall's branch of the United California Bank on the night of
March 17, 1972. It was almost midnight, and the only sign of
life at the mall was the rapidly blinking neon "Bar" sign above
the restaurant a short distance north of the bank. There were
still a few cars in the restaurant's parking lot, but the guard was
nowhere to be seen.

The Oldsmobile circled the bank once more and then
stopped at its rear entrance, out of sight of the parking lot. In
the glare of the headlights, the building looked like a big square
chocolate cake with a layer of frosting across the top. Leaving
the headlights on, the driver opened the trunk and began hauling out tools. Another man removed a ladder from the roof rack
and set it up against the bank's rear wall. A third man, carrying a
shotgun, kept a watchful eye on the surrounding area. Everyone
was wearing dark clothes and brown gloves.

As soon as the ladder was secured, the fourth man climbed
up to inspect the roof. This was Amil Alfred Dinsio, a master
bank robber from Ohio, well known to the FBI. At age 36,
Amil Dinsio was one of the most accomplished bank robbers in
the United States. During the past two decades, he had robbed

at least a dozen banks, but had never been convicted. The FBI claimed that his thefts had already exceeded $30 million.

Despite that notoriety, Dinsio was an unusually quiet man for a bank robber. He rarely said much—especially about his robberies. He was not imposing—if anything, he was the very opposite. Everything about Amil Dinsio was medium. Medium build, medium height, medium weight, average looks—nothing to make him stand out in a crowd. That might have bothered some people, but Dinsio considered it a real professional advantage. Nothing to attract the attention of witnesses. Nothing to draw the notice of the police.

The other unusual thing about Amil Dinsio was his method of bank robbing. There are basically two kinds of bank robbers: the "snatch-and-grabbers" and the "vault bombers." Most grabbers just burst into a bank in broad daylight, waving guns to intimidate the employees and customers, using the element of speed and surprise to snatch whatever cash they can convince the bank's employees to hand over. They do all this in just a few minutes, counting on slow police response times and fast cars to make their getaways. Most bank robbers belong to this category.

The bombers, on the other hand, go after the bank's vault and the contents of its safety deposit boxes. This takes a lot of time and an enormous amount of technical expertise. It requires more people, and usually takes at least two or three days to pull off. Vault bombers do their work at night or on weekends. Their enormous investment in time, money, planning, and organization has made them an increasingly rare breed in bank-robbing circles.

Amil Dinsio was a full-time, totally committed bank vault bomber.

Up on the roof, Dinsio hooded his flashlight and aimed it at various strategic parts of the roof. He liked what he saw. A huge air conditioner that made it easy to stay hidden from the parking lot. Exposed and readily accessible electric wires coming in from a nearby power pole. A flat tarred roof that looked easy to cut through.

"Bring up the tools," he called down in a low voice.

It took him only a few minutes to tap into the bank's electrical cables to power his drill and jigsaw. While one of his men aimed his flashlight at the right spot, Dinsio covered the drill with his jacket to muffle the sound and drilled a test hole into the roof. The drill bit passed through like butter. Inserting the blade of his jigsaw into the hole, Dinsio cut out a section large enough for a man to climb through. Then he lowered in a drop-light on a cord.

As he'd suspected, there was a false ceiling about an arm's length below the roof. This left a service area above it for all the bank's pipes, wires, and air conditioning. It also provided ready access to the top of the bank's vault—visible from this distance as a flat slab of concrete protruding just above the false ceiling. So far, so good.

There were two more details to investigate before he would make his final decision about this bank. First, the vault itself. He lowered himself into the service area and climbed over the pipes and wires to that concrete slab. Here, too, he found pretty much what he'd hoped for—cement that, when he pounded on it, sounded to be about 18 inches (45 cm) thick. Probably reinforced with steel rods an inch (2.5 cm) thick. Very strong, but nothing a few sticks of dynamite wouldn't handle.

Then he looked around for the telephone junction box. There had to be a junction box up here somewhere—builders liked to install them where they weren't visible to the customers. Such a box contained the connections linking the vault alarm to the nearest police station. After several minutes of exploring, Dinsio found that, too. He recognized the brand. He'd disabled that type before. No problem.

Back up on the roof, he positioned the cut-out piece back into place and sealed it around its edges with roofing tar from a caulking tube. Then he signaled the all-clear. The car, which had disappeared, returned. While one of the other men swept up the sawdust and cleared away the equipment, Dinsio stuck a small mirror into the hardening tar and aimed it at a nearby hill to the east. From tomorrow until they hit the bank on the weekend, one of his men would be positioned in those hills with binoculars, watching the reflections from that mirror. If they changed, or the mirror disappeared, they would know that someone had discovered the break-in.

DURING THE NEXT FOUR DAYS, the crew—there were six altogether—hadn't a moment to spare. There was a lot of equipment to buy and assemble: dynamite, blasting caps, sledge hammers, a cutting torch, oxygen and propane tanks, burlap sacks, shovels, all sorts of electrical and electronic gadgetry, aerosol cans of urethane foam, walkie-talkies—the list seemed endless.

But the men knew exactly what to do. Most were from Youngstown, Ohio—Dinsio's hometown—and had worked with Dinsio before. In fact, all but one were related to him by blood or marriage. This was one of the reasons the FBI had always found it impossible to infiltrate Dinsio's operations. Dinsio was big on family. As a rule, the more people who were involved in a bank robbery, the greater the chance of betrayal—but Dinsio had always found that family members were less likely to rat on each other.

Most families wouldn't have included the many kinds of experts that a vault-bombing job required, but Dinsio's family was special. It had a long history of law-breaking. Most of his brothers and uncles were criminals of one sort or another. His cousins had names like "Lips" Moceri, "Crab" Carabbia, and "Animal" Ciasullo. According to one newspaper report, Dinsio's father Amelio, a successful bank robber in his own right, had once conducted a bank-robbing school in Cleveland, Ohio. In fact, the Dinsios owned and operated such a widespread network of criminal enterprises in the Youngstown area that the *Saturday Evening Post* had labeled the city "Crimetown, USA."

Dinsio had chosen the United California Bank at Laguna Niguel because it was located in California's Orange County, one of the most affluent areas in America. Lots of rich, retired people lived in Orange County—and rich, retired people usually kept a lot of cash, gold and silver bullion, and jewelry in their safety deposit boxes. Despite this, Dinsio had discovered that the Orange County sheriff's department had only assigned one full-time and one part-time patrol car to the area.

To provide Dinsio's crew with a base, a Dinsio relative had taken a three-month lease on a condominium in South Gate, a short distance from the bank. It contained a big recreation room that the crew could use as a dormitory, and as a storage and assembly shop. As part of his crew, Dinsio even brought along his wife to cook and act as den mother.

On the night after their initial break-in, Dinsio warned his crew members that there were two things they would have to be careful about when hitting this bank. One was the Monarch Bay Drugstore, which was located right next to the bank—the two businesses shared a common wall. Since the bank's vault was located right up against this common wall, and the drugstore's checkout was located only two paces away from the vault, this meant that no work could be done in the vault during the drugstore's hours of business. Unfortunately, the Monarch Bay Drugstore stayed open all weekend. This gave Dinsio's crew only three nights and no days to get the job done.

The second factor was the mall guard. They had already discovered that he didn't seem to take his job very seriously, but he had to be kept in mind. Two of the men were detailed to discover when he made his rounds, and what his routines might be.

By Friday night, March 24, everything was ready to roll.

Minutes after the drugstore had closed and its employees had driven away, the Oldsmobile reappeared. This time, it was so weighted down with equipment, its tailpipe almost dragged on the pavement.

While the equipment was being unloaded by the light of the headlights, Dinsio set up a police scanner to monitor police radio transmissions. Then he set the ladder against the bank's rear wall again and climbed up to its outdoor alarm bell. The bell was protected by a slotted steel box that couldn't be removed from the outside, but Dinsio had a solution for that. While one of his cousins aimed his flashlight at the box, Dinsio simply poked the nozzle of a can of urethane foam through its slots and sent a surge of foam gushing into the bell's clapper mechanism. Within seconds, the bell's entire innards were immobilized by the fast-hardening foam.

As soon as Dinsio had disabled the bell, everyone got back into the car to monitor the police radio. After 15 minutes of silence, their anxious faces lit only by the glow of the car's dash light, they decided the bell hadn't triggered any alarms.

Next item on the agenda was to disable the vault alarm. This would be a lot trickier. On the roof, Dinsio quickly removed the cut-out piece of the roof and slid down into the bank's service area, pulling the drop-light after him. At the junction box, he gently pulled off the lid and shone the light inside. He spent a long time studying the maze of criss-crossed wires. Then, using a diagram as a guide, he began carefully clipping jumper wires to various terminals, bypassing certain circuits.

As the bypasses multiplied, Dinsio began to sweat.

Outside, everyone held his breath.

Finally Dinsio's head reappeared at the roof's edge. "Done," he said simply.

Once again, everyone gathered at the car to monitor the police radio. This time, they waited a full half hour, in case the police were using special codes. But no police cruiser showed up, and no guard appeared.

"All right," Dinsio said finally. "Looks like we're clear. Let's move!"

While two of the men carried a heavy drill rig onto the roof and wrestled it down into the service area, two more began to shovel dirt into 20 burlap sacks. One man remained on guard at the car, staying in radio contact with the man who was keeping watch from the hill to the east. Dinsio moved from place to place and man to man, keeping an eye on everything.

It was almost midnight before they were able to start drilling into the vault ceiling. Inside the service area, the single drop-light cast the men's long shadows eerily against the back wall. It was so bright it was hard to believe that some of the light wasn't leaking into the empty bank below, but Dinsio had checked it and found everything dark. The sound, however, was another story. Even though they used their jackets to muffle it, there is no way to fully silence a churning concrete drill. After a few minutes, Dinsio had a brainwave: the air conditioner! He climbed down into the bank's lobby to turn it on. That helped mask the sound.

After they had drilled six finger-deep holes into the vault ceiling, they packed them with dynamite and topped them with blasting caps. Then everyone began hauling in the dirt-filled sacks. Nine of the sacks were packed directly over the holes to deflect the force of the blast downward. The other eleven were piled up into a protective barrier some distance away, to shield the trigger-man. When everything was ready, the trigger-man pulled on an oxygen mask and everyone else climbed out onto the roof. They all crouched down behind the air conditioner.

This was the most dangerous part of the whole operation.

It was just after three o'clock in the morning. The restaurant was now closed and empty. The light in the guard's trailer at the other end of the mall was out, and his next security check wasn't scheduled until six o'clock. Dinsio had just talked with the lookout on the hill who'd assured him that nothing looked out of the ordinary from up there.

Dinsio crouched by the hole in the roof. "Okay," he said into the dark. "Any time you're ready."

Two seconds later, there was a loud KABOOM! The bank shook as if it had been hit by an earthquake. A thick cloud of smoke and dust belched out of the roof hole.

The men behind the air conditioner looked around anxiously. It was hard to believe such an explosion could have gone unnoticed, even at this time of night. It was even harder to believe that it wouldn't have woken up the guard. A few lights did come on in the subdivision on the other side of Monarch Bay Road, but they soon went out again. The guard's trailer stayed dark.

Dinsio listened anxiously to the police scanner.

Still nothing. No sirens, no cruisers.

The trigger-man's head popped up out of the roof hole, still masked and now heavily coated in dust and soot. He dragged the mask off his face.

"Better get that exhaust fan going," he said. "It's a stinker in here."

They had to run the exhaust fan for over an hour to get rid of the smoke and the stench of dynamite. Once the air had cleared enough to examine the effects of the blast, Dinsio crawled in and had a look. There was more debris than he had expected, but the blast had done the job. A ragged hole had been blown through the vault ceiling, big enough for a man to climb through. It was still criss-crossed with reinforcing rods, but a cutting torch would make short work of those.

"Looks good," Dinsio reported when he'd climbed back onto the roof. "Let's haul the tanks and torches in there, and then we'll call it a night."

Half an hour later, everyone was back in the apartment, crawling into sleeping bags. Only the lookout on the hill remained at his post, keeping his binoculars trained on the bank.

THE GANG WAITED until 11 o'clock the next night before returning to the bank. This time the parking lot next to the res- taurant was almost full and the action in the bar was brisk. But the shouts of the patrons and the pounding beat of the live band provided plenty of sound cover. And besides, the noisiest part of the robbery was over.

Cutting away the reinforcing rods took less than an hour. By midnight, Amil Dinsio was inspecting the inside of the vault.

What he saw looked mighty promising. The vault was bursting with safety deposit boxes—over 500 of them.

Fifteen minutes later, four of the gang were hard at work in the vault, punching out the deposit box locks with specially tapered hammers. A fifth examined the contents of each box, quickly sifting out the valuables. It wasn't long before the vault floor was knee-deep in discarded parchments and legal documents, photographs, artwork—and more bizarre items like clumps of human hair, false teeth, decayed food, and urns containing human ashes. The valuables were stuffed into burlap sacks and hoisted up through the hole.

As bag after bag of treasure was passed up, the mood in the vault became giddy. One of the men began to sing. Another joined in. The jokes became raucous. This was clearly a major score. This was payoff time.

Several hours later, though, the mood had become more subdued. The air circulation in the tightly confined space had become so bad it was now difficult to breathe. It also became unbearably hot. The men stripped down to their waists and began to work in shifts, taking a breather on the roof every hour or so.

Even so, when dawn came and Dinsio insisted that the work stop—in case the mall guard actually showed up for his six o'clock check—the men climbed out of the vault reluctantly. There were still a few hundred safety deposit boxes to go, and it was hard to resist the temptation to carry on.

Outside, the sun was just beginning to soften the horizon above the Laguna Hills. Birds had begun to sing in the rhododendron bushes along the side of the bank. After the previous night's racket, the restaurant and bar stood closed and shuttered, seemingly abandoned. The parking lot was completely empty.

"One more night, boys," Dinsio said. "One more, and it's a wrap." He turned and waved to the invisible lookout in the hills.

MOST OF SUNDAY the men felt jumpy. The mop-up of a bank robbery could be a dangerous time. It always took a lot longer than expected, and if the score was successful, there was always the chance you'd get too confident, too sloppy.

Plus, it could be really boring. Every piece of equipment had to be wiped down with solvent to remove fingerprints. Every article of clothing had to be washed for the same reason. The walls, furniture, and even the floors of any room that had been used had to be wiped absolutely clean. Every little piece of discarded paper, packaging, or garbage had to be removed.

Some gangs actually hired professionals who specialized in after-crime cleanup, but Dinsio didn't believe in entrusting such important work to strangers. By Sunday afternoon, he had everyone hard at work, getting a head start on it. He was so fussy and obsessive about it that he annoyed everybody.

When they returned to the bank at dusk, everything was as they had left it. While half the gang attacked the last of the deposit boxes, the rest began to clean up the service area. Every surface, every piece of metal or wood that anyone might have touched was given a scrubbing. Dinsio assigned two men with flashlights to search the entire area around the bank to make sure nothing had been dropped or forgotten. "Take a rag and wipe out any tire marks in the dirt alongside the service road, too," he instructed. "One of the worst giveaways is tire marks."

As tools were hauled down to the car and cleaned, they were stashed in a false bottom of the trunk. The burlap sacks of loot were piled in on top.

When the last man had climbed out of the vault, Dinsio climbed back in to do a final double-check.

The vault looked thoroughly ransacked. The floor was knee-deep in crushed paper debris, and the cabinets with their mangled deposit boxes looked as if they'd been hit by a bulldozer. Dinsio looked around for telltale cigarette butts, candy wrappers, toothpicks—anything that might give the police a hint. But everything looked clean.

Before climbing back out, Dinsio smashed the vault's time-lock from the inside. This would make it impossible for the bank's employees to get into the vault on Monday morning, giving the gang another half day or so before the break-in was discovered.

Back at the apartment, they transferred all the loot into packing cases to be shipped to Ohio by truck. Then everyone helped Dinsio's wife with the final wipe-down. The Oldsmobile was stored in the garage of an acquaintance until one of the local gang members could dispose of it and its contents. Everyone shook hands, and the out-of-towners headed for the airport.

It had been a trademark Dinsio heist.

Or had it?

AT 8 O'CLOCK THAT MORNING, the bank's assistant manager arrived ahead of everyone else as usual, to unlock the bank and open the vault.

The bank doors unlocked just fine, but the vault door seemed to be jammed.

The assistant manager twirled the combination dial again and again. The door wouldn't budge.

By 10 o'clock, when even a locksmith had been unable to solve the problem, a service technician from the vault manufacturer was called. He worked on the lock until mid-afternoon before giving up.

Eventually, the technician suggested that the only option left was to drill into the vault ceiling from the service area. He led the way through a hatch in the bank's false ceiling to show the manager what he meant.

That's when the $8 million break-in of the Laguna Niguel branch of the United California Bank was finally discovered.

THE POLICE AND THE FBI were immediately notified. A crowd of officers and agents swarmed through the bank. Evidence was examined, sorted, and cross-checked. Employees, security personnel, and even customers were interviewed. Every conceivable surface was dusted for fingerprints.

No luck.

Not a smidgen of luck.

Over a hundred police officers and agents worked on the case for over two months without one useful result.

And that's where the story might have ended—another picture-perfect Dinsio bank robbery—except that a mere two months later, Dinsio robbed a bank in Lordstown, Ohio, using the same crew and the identical method he had used for the Laguna Niguel heist.

Being in Dinsio's home state, the Lordstown police were familiar with his methods and immediately suspected him. Although they couldn't arrest him—like the Laguna Niguel robbery, the one in Lordstown was frustratingly "clean"—they informed the FBI of their suspicions, and the FBI immediately saw the similarities. The FBI still had no hard evidence, either— but now they had a name.

They began by asking all commercial airlines flying into

Los Angeles to check their records for an Amil Dinsio. To their astonishment, they hit paydirt. For some reason, Dinsio had flown to Los Angeles on his way to Laguna Niguel under his own name!

Then they managed to find the cabbie who had taken Dinsio and his crew to their rented South Gate apartment. The cabbie remembered the place, and took the police to the address. The apartment was still empty—the lease had only just ended, and a new tenant hadn't yet been found.

The police immediately searched and dusted the entire apartment. Nothing—as usual. But then someone made an incredible discovery. *The dishwasher had been filled, but not run.* It was still full of unwashed dishes! Those dishes gave the FBI an excellent collection of prints from the entire gang.

The police then checked out every phone call the gang had made from this apartment. It included the man in whose garage the Oldsmobile had been stored—stored and unwisely not yet disposed of. A search of the car turned up many of the gang's tools—*and* a few jewels that had dropped unnoticed out of one of the burlap sacks.

Checkmate!

It took the FBI another year to make their case legally watertight, but once they did it was game over for Dinsio and his gang. Almost all of them got 20 years in the slammer.

And the moral of the story? No job is completed until the dishes are done!

Take the Money and Fly

IT WAS 4:45 on the evening of Wednesday, November 24, 1971. Northwest Airlines Flight 305 had just reached cruising altitude on its short hop from Portland, Oregon to Seattle, Washington. There were 36 passengers onboard, plus a three-man flight crew and two stewardesses.

The call button above seat 15D lit up and a chime rang in the galley. Stewardess Florence Schaffner went forward to investigate.

The only passenger in Row 15—to all appearances an ordinary businessman—had black hair and seemed middle-aged. He was wearing a dark suit and tinted glasses. He held out a folded note.

"Would you read this, please?" he asked politely.

Schaffner hesitated. This was one of the challenges of being a flight attendant—how to refuse requests for a date without being rude.

The man sensed her resistance. "It's very important," he insisted. "Please read it now."

Schaffner sighed and unfolded the note.

The message, printed in handwritten letters, read: *I have a bomb in my briefcase. I will require $200,000 in $20 bills and four parachutes. These items must be delivered to me at Seattle Airport as soon as we land. If these demands are not met, I will blow up this aircraft.*

Schaffner blanched. She rushed up to the cockpit, the note flapping in her hand.

AT FIRST, the flight crew thought it was a bad joke. In the 1970s, commercial airline hijackings were virtually unknown on North America's west coast. The only ones that had happened had been on the eastern side of the continent, on flights heading to the Middle East or Europe—and even these had been very rare.

"It's got to be a hoax," Captain William Scott said. "I'll go talk to him." He turned to his co-pilot. "You take the controls, Bob."

The rest of the crew watched as Scott walked back to Row 15 and sat down in 15C, across the aisle. The hijacker leaned over and the two talked in voices too low to hear. At one point, the man reached under his seat and hauled up a briefcase, opening it briefly. When Scott returned to the cockpit, his expression was grave.

"He's serious," he said. "He's got some red cylinders wired together in his briefcase that could be a bomb. Get me Seattle traffic control, Bob."

For the next 20 minutes, increasingly urgent radio messages flashed back and forth across the Pacific Northwest. Seattle traffic control called the Seattle police. The Seattle police called the FBI. The FBI called Northwest Airlines president Donald Nyrop.

What should they do? Refuse the hijacker's demands in hopes that the bomb was a fake? Try to overpower the man in the air? Pretend to cooperate and then storm the plane when it landed?

It was Donald Nyrop's call.

At 5:05 p.m.—as Flight 305 began to descend toward Seattle Airport—Scott finally received a radio message from Nyrop. "Give him anything he wants," it said.

But it wasn't going to be that easy. The hijacker now informed Scott that he wasn't allowing the plane to land before the money and the parachutes were ready for pickup.

"But we're on final approach," Scott protested.

"Then abort it," the hijacker ordered.

"Be reasonable," Scott pleaded. "We haven't got a lot of extra fuel."

"You've got half an hour's worth of extra fuel," the hijacker said calmly. "Just tell the police to hurry up."

This was the FBI's first indication that this hijacker had really done his homework.

As Flight 305 locked into a holding pattern over Seattle airport, FBI agents scrambled frantically to gather the money and the chutes.

By now, they had determined that the hijacker had checked in at Portland International Airport under the name of Dan Cooper. It was also increasingly clear that he had planned his heist with impressive care. With 41 passengers in an airliner circling above Seattle on a limited amount of fuel, the FBI had no time to mark or booby-trap the ransom money the way they usually did. And they couldn't sabotage the parachutes, either. In demanding four of them, Cooper had given the FBI no alternative but to assume there was a chance that some of the flight crew might be forced to use them, too.

BY THE TIME THE AGENTS had assembled the money and the parachutes, Flight 305 had been circling Seattle airport for over half an hour. Its tanks were almost dry.

"We're ready down here," traffic control radioed at 5:34 p.m. "Come on in."

At 5:40 p.m., Northwest Flight 305 finally landed safely at the Seattle-Tacoma Airport. Most of its passengers were ignorant of the ordeal they had just been through.

Once the plane had rolled to a stop, Cooper ordered Scott, his flight crew, and one stewardess to squeeze into the cockpit and shut the door. Then he let the passengers and the second stewardess get off. As an FBI agent climbed up the ramp with the parachutes and a canvas bag filled with money, Cooper crouched out of the line of fire and kept one hand clamped inside his briefcase. He ordered everything dropped just inside the aircraft door and the agent to withdraw. Then he closed the door.

"Fuel up the plane," he told Captain Scott as he let everyone back out of the cockpit. "Get flight clearance for a low-altitude course from Seattle to Reno. I want you to fly no higher than 10,000 feet and no faster than 150 knots an hour. Keep your flaps and landing gear down, and the cabin unpressurized. And Captain," he added, as if he could read Scott's mind, "I'll know if my instructions aren't being followed. I'm wearing an altimeter."

Captain Scott had noticed that.

It was becoming clear to him what Cooper had in mind. Ten thousand feet (about 3000 m) was the highest altitude from which a parachutist could safely jump without oxygen. And, of all the commercial airliners flown in North America, only a Boeing 727 could fly as slow as 150 knots (250 kph) without stalling. It was also the only airliner with a rear door that could be opened during flight. Plus, a 727's rear door and engines were positioned in such a way that they wouldn't endanger an exiting parachutist.

The fact was, the 727 wouldn't have been more perfect for such a hijacking if it had been specifically designed for it!

AS THE PLANE REGAINED ALTITUDE, Cooper peered through the aircraft's windows to assure himself that the Cascade Mountains were on his right, and the Rockies on his left—proof that his instructions were being followed. When his altimeter showed 10,000 feet, he ordered everyone into the cockpit and once again closed the door. Now the flight crew could no longer see what he was doing.

In the galley at the rear of the plane, Cooper transferred some chocolate bars and apples from his briefcase into the money bag. Then he used a damp towel from the galley to wipe down any surfaces he might have touched. Finally, he belted the money bag across his chest, buckled himself into one of the parachutes, and eased open the rear door.

A blast of wet air roared into the passenger cabin, sending papers and plastic bags flying. A sign designating the door as an emergency exit tore away and was sucked out into the night. Up in the cockpit, a red warning light lit up, indicating a door had been opened during flight. "Is everything all right back there?" Captain Scott called over the intercom. "Can we help you with anything?"

"No," Cooper called back.

That was the last word anyone heard from him.

The plane flew on, silent and without incident, all the way to Reno. Two F-106 fighter jets that had been ordered into the sky from a nearby air force base zoomed past several times, unable to fly slow enough to keep an eye on the airliner, to determine if or when Cooper had jumped. There was by now so much low cloud and rain in the area that the crew of a National

Guard helicopter giving chase never even saw the 727, and the pilot of a slow-flying National Guard T-33 Trainer couldn't find it until it was well over Oregon. Once he had it in his sights, the Trainer dogged the airliner all the way across the Oregon-California border, but the pilot reported nothing out of the ordinary.

From interviews with the flight crew and passengers, the FBI quickly produced an artist's conception of what Cooper looked like. They distributed a "Wanted" poster throughout the US Postal system. Newspapers, television newscasts, and radio stations picked up the story, and for the next several days it was headline news. Due to a mix-up, an FBI spokesman mistakenly identified the hijacker as "D.B. Cooper," and that's the name by which he became known to the public. Tips, hunches, and suggestions poured into FBI offices all over the United States. Search planes flew the entire 600-mile (1000-km) route between Seattle and Reno, duplicating the airliner's flight path.

None of these efforts produced a single useful lead. D.B. Cooper—or whatever his name was—seemed to have vanished from the face of the earth.

Several days later, an idea occurred to Captain Scott. He suggested dumping a package weighing roughly the same as a man and a parachute out of the back door of a 727 in flight, to see if its sensitive flight instruments would register such a "jump." If they did, technicians could then check Flight 305's November 24 flight recorder to find out exactly when a similar jump might have happened during its Seattle-to-Reno flight. That would allow them to determine at least the general area where the vanished hijacker might have landed.

Would a man jumping out of a 150,000-pound (69,000-kg) airliner have made much of a difference to its flight settings?

Not likely—but the FBI was becoming desperate, and decided to give it a try.

They loaded a 727 with a package weighing 180 pounds (82 kg), took it up to an altitude of 10,000 feet (3000 m) over the ocean, and opened its rear door. They maneuvered the package into the doorway, waited until the pilot gave the signal, and then pushed it out into the open sky.

As the package tumbled off the plane, the plane bobbed slightly. Its autopilot instantly trimmed back the flaps just a touch.

"We got it!" the pilot shouted.

Finally, some progress!

Back on the ground, the technicians hurried over to Northwest's flight operations office with the plane's "black box"—the sealed recorder that keeps an electronic record of all the airplane's maneuvers throughout a flight. Four hours later, Donald Nyrop got the call.

Flight 305's flight recorder showed that the airliner's autopilot had trimmed back the plane's flaps in exactly the same manner on November 24, just as the plane had passed over Cowlitz and Clark counties, about 40 miles (65 km) northeast of Vancouver, Washington. This was a heavily forested area near the Lewis River, in the heart of Washington's logging country. Calculating the direction and strength of the winds in this area for November 24 to determine the drift of Cooper's parachute, the FBI decided that the area around the town of Ariel, Washington was the most likely place Cooper might have landed.

Within days, a flotilla of aircraft, boats, and jeeps descended on the town. Over 300 soldiers, police, FBI agents, and volunteers swarmed through the surrounding forest, interviewing loggers, plowing through underbrush, floating down creeks and rivers, and making reconnaissance flights. They were all looking, in the words of one pilot, "for a parachute or a hole." Excitement built quickly when a pilot saw what appeared to be a parachute hanging from a spruce tree, but unfortunately it turned out to be a deflated weather balloon. A large piece of orange fabric in a meadow sent expectations soaring, but turned out to be a tarp-covered teepee. Several bodies were even discovered, but none turned out to be that of D.B. Cooper.

Finally, after 18 days of futile searching, a heavy snowstorm brought the operation to an end.

This didn't, however, close the FBI's file on Dan Cooper. The following spring, they mounted a similar operation covering almost double the previous area, using an even larger battalion of soldiers from nearby Fort Lewis.

They had no luck this time, either.

Then, a full eight years later, three hikers strolling along a logging road in Cowlitz County found the remains of an emergency door exit sign that appeared to have been sucked out of an airliner. The FBI were able to confirm that it had indeed come out of a 727. That, at least, suggested that investigators were on the right track.

A year later, an eight-year-old boy named Brian Ingram caused tremendous excitement and briefly became famous when he found $5,800 in two bundles of badly faded $20 bills on the banks of the Columbia River, just northwest of Vancouver, Washington. The FBI had the sodden money analyzed in an FBI lab in Washington, DC. It proved to be part of the Cooper money. The FBI promptly hired archeology students to dig further trenches in the area where the boy had found the money, and a third bundle was found. It, too, checked out as Cooper money.

But since then, the trail has gone cold. Although hundreds of treasure-seekers continued to dig in the area where the money was found, no further banknotes or evidence of any other kind has ever turned up.

As of this telling, D.B. Cooper remains uncaught—the only hijacking extortionist in American history ever to successfully evade the FBI's efforts to bring him to justice. His file remains open, and his case officially unsolved.

SO WHAT *DID* HAPPEN to Dan Cooper? Did he survive his parachute jump and live to enjoy his ill-gotten gains, as some investigators believe? Or was he killed on landing, or perhaps wounded to die of exposure in the wilderness of southwestern Washington? At least half a dozen books have addressed this question, as well as a popular song, several movies, and a play. Each one is full of speculations, theories, and a lot of just plain guesswork.

Perhaps the most convincing explanation became available in 1983, when Max Gunther, a New York journalist, received a call from a woman who gave her name as Clara.

Clara explained that she had recently lost her husband, a man she called Paul Cotton. Paul had been a great fan of Max Gunther's articles, she said, and so it was to Gunther that she wished to offer Paul Cotton's rather extraordinary story.

"Just how extraordinary?" Gunther wanted to know. He was often pestered by people who felt he simply had to tell their amazing stories to the world.

"He was Dan Cooper, the skyjacker," Clara said.

Gunther chuckled. "Well, you certainly have my attention," he said. "But I have to warn you, I'm going to be pretty hard to convince."

As Clara told her husband's story and readily answered

Gunther's increasingly probing questions, Gunther became convinced that she might be telling the truth. She knew many details that had never been published, details that the FBI had kept secret in order to test people like Clara. She knew that the name on the flight ticket had been Dan Cooper rather than D.B. Cooper. She knew exactly what Cooper had been wearing on the night of the hijacking, and was able to correct a number of facts that the FBI had misreported or misunderstood. She knew the color of his parachute's canopy and where he had buried it. She knew why only a small number of the ransom banknotes had been found on the banks of the Columbia River.

After a number of such grillings, Gunther decided to test Clara's story against his own exhaustive investigation. The result was a book, published in 1985, entitled *D.B. Cooper: What Really Happened*.

ACCORDING TO CLARA, Captain Scott's calculations were remarkably accurate. Cooper had indeed jumped out of the airliner over Clark County near the Lewis River, into a blinding rainstorm with freezing temperatures and a 70 mile per hour (115 kph) wind. An experienced paratrooper who had served a stint in the US Army, Cooper let himself fall toward earth at a breathtaking 120 miles per hour (200 kph), resisting the urge to pull his ripcord until his altimeter showed just over 3,000 feet (1000 m).

The wind was calmer at this altitude, but when Cooper finally released his chute, it still slammed open so violently that it almost felt as if he'd hit a mountaintop. Seconds later, he emerged out of heavy rainclouds, upwind of a cluster of lights that seemed to be a town. He steered his chute toward those lights.

So far, so good. His plan was to land far enough out of town to avoid being seen, then bury his parachute and suit jacket. What stewardess Schaffner had described as his "stocky build" had actually been a heavy sweater under his dress shirt; heavy sweaters and backpacks (even when filled with banknotes) tended to pass unnoticed in logging towns. He'd spent enough time exploring this area to make sure about that sort of thing.

Suddenly, a branch flashed past on his left. Another branch, then another. Damn! He'd become distracted; he was lower than he thought. Too late now to prepare for a proper five-point landing. He hit the ground with a strangled yelp as a searing stab of pain shot through his right ankle. He bounced and rolled clumsily, his face plowing into a thick layer of wet leaves. He felt the sodden canopy of the parachute collapse against the back of his head.

He sat up, pushed away the fabric and cords, and spat out the leaves in his mouth.

The night was so black he couldn't see a thing. All he could hear was the wind roaring in the trees and churning water nearby.

The pain in his ankle was bad, seriously bad, but there was nothing he could do about it at this time of night. That would have to wait until morning. He pulled the parachute over himself like a sleeping bag and tried to sleep.

At dawn, the rain was still falling and the sky was a dark, glowering gray. All around him, huge cedar and hemlock trees creaked and moaned. Cooper's clothes were drenched, and his ankle felt a lot worse. He gasped as he pulled himself up to survey the situation.

His first attempt to put weight on his right foot produced such a severe flash of pain, he cried out in agony.

It took him almost an hour to find and cut himself a walking stick. Then he pulled a wad of banknotes out of the canvas bag and distributed them among his pockets. He buried the bag and the rest of the money, the chute, and the suit jacket in a shallow hole under a nearby log. By the time he was able to begin a slow hobble toward the town, he was so exhausted with pain he felt on the verge of passing out.

He didn't make it all the way to town. Near a cabin on a gravel road about a mile (1.6 km) from Ariel's outskirts, he found a toolshed with its door unlocked. It was as far as he could go. He dragged himself into the shed and barely managed to close its door before he lost consciousness completely.

AS A CHILD, Clara had been the baby of the family, and her parents had never learned to treat her any other way. They had refused to let her date boys, accept a scholarship from an out-of-state college, or take up her best friend's offer of work and a shared apartment in New York City after graduation. Although she had always dreamed of escaping her family's control, Clara had never developed the self-confidence to try. So she had settled for a loveless marriage and a job as a secretary, neither of which had lasted for very long.

In November 1971, at the age of 37, she was living alone in her uncle's cabin on the Lewis River, babysitting the uncle's dog while he was overseas.

On the morning of November 26, the dog seemed to find the toolshed in the cabin's backyard enormously exciting. He sniffed and barked and whined at its door as if he'd cornered a skunk or a raccoon in there.

Clara went out to investigate.

Instead of a raccoon, she found a dark-eyed, dark-haired

stranger lying on the toolshed floor. He was wet, in obvious pain, and had just regained consciousness.

CLARA OFTEN MARVELED—then, and for years afterwards—that she didn't follow her first impulse and call the local sheriff. There was something about this man's calm manner, his mild voice, and his obvious helplessness that eased her fear. So instead of calling the authorities, she helped him into her cabin and made him some tea.

She surprised herself even more a few hours later by driving him to a local doctor and, as his broken ankle was being splinted, telling the doctor he was a visiting cousin.

In the doctor's washroom, she caught sight of herself in the mirror and realized she hadn't thought about how she looked to other people for a long time. She seemed to herself presentable enough: round-faced, medium height, glasses, dark-haired. But average, very average. Maybe not all that interesting. Was that how he saw her, too?

And why on earth did she care? She didn't even know this man.

He'd told her his name was Paul Cotton, and that he was from California, but he'd been vague about what he was doing here and how he'd hurt himself. She suspected he was on the run from something. He did, once they'd returned to her cabin, mention something about bad debts. But mostly he was curious about her. Clara found him so easy to talk to, it didn't take long before she was telling him her whole story.

He listened quietly, attentively. He didn't seem to find her boring at all. His questions were gentle and encouraging.

In time, he revealed a little more about himself. He described a childhood in Canada and teenage years in New Jersey. A stint in the US Army as a paratrooper after high school; uninspired college grades, a boring marriage, two kids. His career as a salesman, a house in the suburbs. And his eventual decision to chuck it all.

She felt she knew exactly what he was talking about. She too felt caught in a web of mediocrity, of being underestimated, undervalued. She too was tired of being nothing special to anyone.

They were watching the news on television when the FBI's drawing of D.B. Cooper flashed onto the screen.

"They've been running that story for a couple of days now," she said idly.

And suddenly the possibility that the man in the drawing and the man beside her were the same person hit her so strongly, she knew immediately that she must have suspected it for some time.

She gasped. And then she asked him, quickly, before she lost her nerve: "Are you the hijacker? The man they're calling D.B. Cooper?"

To her astonishment, he didn't even try to deny it.

"My lord," she said, dropping her head into her hands. "What do we do now?"

He sat unmoving on the couch where she'd settled him, his splinted leg propped up on her coffee table.

"I guess that's up to you, Clara," he said.

What happened, over the next several weeks, is that Paul and Clara fell in love.

They discovered, to their surprise, that they were a remarkably good fit. Paul's quiet, supportive manner was exactly what Clara needed to develop self-confidence. Clara's admiration for Paul's ingenuity and daring made him feel that he wasn't just an average guy. And, of course, though neither admitted it at the time, the danger they suddenly found themselves in gave their relationship an extra measure of excitement.

Their situation was definitely becoming dangerous. Only a few weeks later, in mid-December, a sudden wave of soldiers and FBI agents swarmed through the town, searching for D.B. Cooper. Everyone in the area was questioned. The local newspaper was filled with the story. The town talked of little else. Paul hid in Clara's attic for days at a time.

Every night, the television broadcast new FBI assurances that they were closing in on the hijacker.

But by some miracle, the doctor who had splinted Paul's leg didn't make the connection. Neither did his nurse, or the few people who may have seen him in Clara's car as she drove him to the doctor.

Then a strong winter blizzard blew a thick blanket of snow over everything, obliterating all tracks and making further access to the area's forest impossible. The soldiers packed up and left, and the FBI agents followed. Normal life returned to the town of Ariel. Paul climbed down from his attic.

The two lovers spent a contented Christmas together. Not long after, they decided it was probably safe enough to go dig up Paul's money.

But when they got to the place, the money was gone.

AT FIRST, Paul thought he might have become confused; in all this snow, it was easy to lose one's bearings. But after some more digging, he found his parachute.

After several more hours of digging, they finally gave up. Someone had obviously discovered the cache and made off with the money. The thief had had his loot stolen.

They were sitting on a log, feeling exhausted and depressed, when Paul saw a raccoon sniffing around the holes they had made. Suddenly, he remembered the apple and chocolate bars he'd packed into the canvas money bag. Could there be a connection? Raccoons, he knew, liked to wash their food before eating it. There was a creek nearby.

He explained his idea to Clara, and they began to search the banks of the creek. Half an hour later, they found the bag.

It had been chewed open and the food taken out. A lot of the money was missing, too. They dug around in the snow and began to find sodden bundles of it, muddy and torn. They recovered $96,000 in soggy bills. Together with the banknotes Paul had taken with him earlier, that made $158,000.

SO NOW PAUL AND CLARA WERE RICH, but only in theory. The FBI hadn't had time to mark the bills, but they'd published their serial numbers. It wasn't terribly likely that bank tellers would examine every $20 bill that passed through their hands, but Paul didn't want to take a chance. The two of them sat around night after night, brainstorming, trying to figure out how they could possibly turn their theoretical fortune into a real one.

In the end, they decided to leave Ariel and head for New York City. Surely in a city that big they would find ways to solve this problem.

But when they arrived in New York, they were startled to find that the D.B. Cooper story hadn't died. In fact, they'd only been in the city a few days when Paul passed a teenager on the street wearing a T-shirt that read *D.B. COOPER, WHERE ARE YOU?* Not long after, the ballad singer Tom Bresh released a popular song about the hijacking that played on the radio for months, and shortly after that the FBI released a new drawing of D.B. Cooper. (Fortunately, it was even less accurate than their original one.)

Four years later, the money was still locked in a suitcase in the basement, and beginning to look as if it might just stay there forever.

By now, Paul and Clara had both found jobs, so they were able to pay their bills. But working nine to five and just managing to make ends meet wasn't exactly the life they'd fantasized for themselves in the little cabin on the Lewis River. That suitcase full of money in the basement was supposed to transform their nondescript lives into something special, something exceptional. That wasn't happening.

And then, in 1976, Paul finally solved the problem.

Casinos!

A friend who'd recently returned from Las Vegas expressed surprise at the huge amounts of cash that poured through the casinos there. On his next business trip to Nevada, Paul took along a bundle of banknotes, bought $50,000 worth of chips, played for an hour (winning $500), then cashed out. The casino paid him back in beautiful, unidentifiable, $50 bills.

The spell on the money in their New York basement had finally been broken.

PAUL AND CLARA wasted little time in getting to work on their dream. In 1976, $158,000 wasn't going to buy them palaces and yachts, but it was enough to pay for a lovely home on New York State's Long Island, in a community that welcomed them with open arms. Though neither had been popular in their previous lives, they now found themselves becoming popular together. They made a lot of friends. They joined clubs and charities. Their home became a regular gathering place for the community.

Their own relationship flourished, too. Paul romanced Clara with flowers and chocolates. They shared a passion for reading and movies. They took leisurely holidays together.

Was it all too good to last?

Sometimes Clara allowed herself to worry a little about that. Sometimes she found herself wondering whether it was right to enjoy so much happiness when it had been bought with a suitcaseful of stolen money.

It was the only thing she and Paul never talked about.

AND THEN, LATE IN 1980, a shadow fell over their lives. A personnel clerk discovered that the college degree Paul had claimed in his job application was bogus. Paul had never even been enrolled at that college.

Paul was fired. He never recovered from this blow. Without letters of reference, he couldn't find another job. He became moody and depressed.

And then, a year later, still no closer to finding a job despite hundreds of applications and dozens of interviews, Paul suddenly—unaccountably—cheered up.

Clara couldn't understand it. It made no sense—until she discovered he'd been spending his days at the airport. "Just watching the planes," he said.

Clara's heart sank. She asked him anxiously whether he was going to "do it again."

He didn't deny it. But he wouldn't discuss it, either.

Their life together collapsed. Clara found it impossible to eat or sleep. She saw disaster looming and she felt helpless to do anything about it.

Clara's fears were well founded. In early 1972, the Boeing Aircraft Company had modified the 727 to make another Cooper-style hijacking impossible. The rear door could no longer be opened during flight. The cockpit door was now equipped with a porthole. Three men who had tried to commit copycat hijackings, in three subsequent attempts, had all been shot.

But Dan Cooper, or Paul Cotton, or whoever he was, never got the chance to attempt another hijacking. He died of a heart attack soon after his admission to Clara.

The FBI acknowledged that Clara's story was compelling and to all appearances convincing. However, they refused to accept it until she identified herself to them in person, and permitted them to question her. This she refused to do. She told Max Gunther that she mistrusted the FBI, and also feared a negative reaction from her family. As of this writing, Clara has retreated into silence, and the FBI continues to consider the case officially "unsolved."

Hitting "Big Daddy"

MOST BANKS HAVE VAULTS, and some of the larger ones have vaults the size of entire houses—but the biggest money vault in the western world is located at the corner of 14th and C Streets in Washington, DC. Here, in a vast building complex covering several square blocks, the US Treasury's Bureau of Engraving & Printing produces, stores, and distributes the hundreds of billions of US dollars needed to run the world's largest economy.

In the almost 100 years of its existence, this astonishing treasure vault—known in the criminal underworld as "Big Daddy"—had never been burgled. Not one of America's most famous bank robbers had ever dared to tackle its formidable security systems. Not one of America's most ingenious burglars had ever tried to breach its rigorously guarded exterior.

Until December 30, 1953. That's when an ordinary, law-abiding, baseball-coaching father of two named James Landis decided to give it a try.

Landis worked for the Bureau of Engraving & Printing. He'd worked there for 10 years—ever since being discharged from the army in 1943, after being wounded twice during the Second World War. None of his supervisors at the Bureau had ever complained about his work, his attitude, or his honesty. His army record was exemplary; he'd made it to the level of sergeant, and had earned a Purple Heart, a Bronze Star, and several

Good Conduct medals. His friends and neighbors in the town of Chapel Oaks all thought of him as a good, reliable family man.

But sometimes—as the famous saying goes—the difference between a thief and an honest man is nothing more than a little matter called "opportunity."

It all started when Landis volunteered to coach a local sandlot baseball team. Attendance at the team's games had been poor, and Landis decided to fix that. He convinced a local printing company to donate printed handbills advertising the team and the dates of its games. The handbills turned out to be exactly the same size as dollar bills, and when the season ended Landis had a boxful of them left over.

At first, as a gag, Landis sandwiched a sheaf of these handbills between two twenty-dollar bills and swaggered around Chapel Oaks' bars and nightclubs, making sure all his friends saw the huge size of his "flash-roll." He got a big kick out of how impressed they were.

Then a less innocent idea occurred to him. If stuffing these handbills between real banknotes looked genuine enough to fool his friends, maybe they could be substituted for real banknotes back at the Bureau where he worked.

Landis's job at the Bureau was quite modest: he carried bricks of banknotes from the Packaging Room to the Currency Vault. Each brick was put together in the Assembly Room, where 4,000 banknotes were pressed tightly between two wooden blocks. Then the entire brick, including the blocks, was banded lengthwise with two steel bands. In the Packaging Room, each brick was wrapped in heavy brown paper and sealed at both ends—one with an offical Treasury seal, the other with a label describing the denomination, serial numbers, print date, and the packer's initials. Landis then carried these wrapped bricks over to the Vault, from which they were distributed to Federal Reserve banks all over the country.

Not much opportunity there. The sequence of bricks was carefully monitored as they passed through the system, and any missing brick would soon be noticed. No chance of substituting a wad of handbills for some real banknotes either, since the bills were packed in sequences that were checked and initialed by individual packers. Any missing bill would be charged back to the responsible packer, and anyway, Landis's job was too far down the assembly line to give him access to individual banknotes.

But over the years, Landis had discovered that there was one flaw in the system that *did* amount to an opportunity.

In addition to all the regular assembly line inspections, Bureau inspectors also made periodic checks of the bricks already stored in the Vault. They selected and broke these open at random, a few at a time, recounting the bills, confirming the count, initialing them, and returning the bundles to the Packaging Room for re-assembly. Any brick missing out of sequence in the Vault was first assumed to have been inspected and returned to the Packaging Room. Checks for these missing bricks were made at the Vault twice a day. If the system was working properly, every out-of-sequence brick should have been repackaged and returned to the Vault by the next check.

Which gave Landis, by his calculation, a window of roughly 6 to 8 hours. Not as much as he would have liked—but probably enough for what he had in mind.

ON THE MORNING of December 29, 1953, James Landis timed his arrival at the Bureau for 7:15 a.m., when the largest crowd of workers poured through the gates. Under his arm, he carried a bag with two fake money bricks, each comprised of a fat wad of his banknote-sized handbills clamped between appropriately sized wooden blocks. Each was wrapped in a square of the Bureau's regulation brown wrapping paper that Landis had sneaked home under his shirt. The rule was that all packages had to be examined by a guard in the parcel booth or left in a locker there, but Landis was hoping that during this holiday season the security would be a little less strict.

No such luck. The guard at the gate spotted the bag immediately. He pointed at it, then to the parcel booth.

Landis nodded and obediently headed toward the booth. He could always just leave the bag in a locker and try again another day. But when the gate guard turned away to monitor new arrivals, Landis quickly changed direction and passed through the employee entry door, bypassing the booth. His hair stood on end and sweat broke out on his forehead as he forced himself to walk calmly down the corridor, expecting every second to hear loud shouts of "Stop! Hey, stop!" But no one challenged him.

He let his shoulders relax a little and wiped his sleeve across his forehead. He passed the Packaging Room, where his shift would start in 15 minutes, and turned up a set of stairs to a third-floor men's room that was out of the way and rarely used.

Here, he quickly hid his fake bricks in the bottom of a garbage bin. Then he hurried back downstairs. In the locker room next to the Packaging Room, he rapidly changed from his street clothes into his work uniform.

In the Packaging Room, he began loading money bricks onto the platform in front of the wrapping machine. Today they were wrapping bricks of $20 bills—each brick worth a whopping $80,000. Landis had carefully timed his heist to occur on a "$20 day."

By 7:50 a.m., the platform was fully loaded. Now he had 20 minutes before it would have to be fully loaded again.

Glancing around casually, he picked up a torn piece of wrapping paper and headed for the garbage bin. But instead of dropping it in the bin, he picked up two bricks of just-wrapped banknotes and folded the paper over them. Keeping his back to the room, he walked purposefully out the door and down the corridor to the elevator. Inside the elevator, he punched the button for the basement.

Casing the building some months earlier, Landis had found a storeroom containing broken and cast-off office furniture. The dust everywhere suggested it hadn't been used in some time. Landis headed for this storeroom now, ducked inside, and locked the door.

He stood motionless in the silent room. He could hear the faint whining of hydraulics, and the occasional shout from the floor above. That, and his own ragged breathing. Calm down, he told himself sternly. Take it easy. It's okay, you can do this.

He set the bricks down on the floor, clamped his feet tightly around one of them, grasped a steel band with a pair of wire-cutting pliers, and squeezed. The band sprang off and the blocks twisted slightly. Landis grasped the second band and squeezed again. With a loud *twang!* it leaped away, the blocks shot forward, and a great shower of banknotes exploded against his face and through the air. Bright, crisp, brand-new $20 bills scattered all over the room. What a sight!

He clamped his feet around the second brick and repeated the operation. The second explosion scattered banknotes even farther, right to the opposite wall. One hundred and sixty thousand dollars' worth of spanking new 20s! It was more than he could earn in 30 years. It was enough to buy 10 houses!

It was an unbelievable fortune.

He glanced at his watch and saw that it was 8:00 a.m. In five minutes, he had to be back in the Packaging Room.

He quickly gathered the banknotes into two large paper bags and shoved them under a low platform that had been pushed against the back of the room. Then he hurried down the corridor.

By 8:05 a.m., Landis was back at his workstation, loading busily. To his immense relief, no one questioned his absence or commented on it.

FOR THE NEXT PART OF HIS PLAN, Landis had calculated he might need anywhere from 15 to 20 minutes, so a similar absence from the platform wouldn't work. He had to wait until his coffee break at 10:40 a.m. The next two and a half hours dragged on at an agonizingly slow pace.

Finally the buzzer rang for coffee break.

Landis hastened back down to the storage room where he had also left the brown paper packaging from the two authentic bricks. He folded these papers up and placed them under his shirt, being careful not to damage their official seals. Then he took the elevator up to the third floor, to the men's room.

It was empty. His luck was holding.

He now had to soak the seals and labels off the authentic packaging, dry them on the radiator, and glue them onto the ends of his two fake bricks. Fortunately, the winter had been colder than usual and all the radiators in the building were on. Once the seals and labels were dry, Landis pulled out a small bottle of glue and attached the seals in the proper places. He was just pressing the last seal into place when he heard footsteps.

He froze.

The footsteps came closer.

Landis clutched the paper, glue, bricks, and bag to his chest and lunged for a cubicle. The washroom door creaked and footsteps entered. Multiple footsteps.

They stopped, and there was a rush of water from a faucet.

"What the devil's that smell?" a voice demanded.

"Smells like rubber cement," someone replied.

The paper towel dispenser rattled, and there was another burst of water.

"Must've had the plumbers in here," the first voice said.

The second voice just grunted.

The footsteps receded and the door creaked shut.

After a moment Landis emerged from his cubicle, his face pale. His hands shook as he pulled another paper towel from the dispenser to wipe off the splashes of water the men had left on the counter. He set down his bricks, then opened the washroom door slightly and peered anxiously up and down the corridor.

Empty again.

Relieved, he returned to the counter to add the final feature he needed to avoid discovery: an additional date stamp on the bricks' labels, to make them look as if they'd been pulled out of sequence by an inspector. He applied this date with a rotary date stamp he'd stolen from the Packaging Room, then added a squiggle of fictitious inspector's initials. Now his bricks were ready to be "returned" to the assembly line, and it didn't matter that they'd be out of sequence, since the restamped date and initials covered that.

At 10:55 a.m., Landis returned to the Packaging Room and added his two fake bricks to a pile of others ready to be hauled to the Vault.

No one paid any attention.

AT NOON, Landis joined his co-workers in the cafeteria but he ate very little. Someone commented on how quiet he was being today. Someone else asked him if he was going to waste that orange. Landis replied and nodded and shrugged, but he felt like a sleepwalker. Numb and slightly breathless—was that how sleepwalkers felt? He wasn't sure; he'd never sleepwalked. All he knew was that he was feeling breathless and terrified and numb and elated, all at the same time.

And the job wasn't finished yet.

The afternoon felt as if he had a giant ball and chain fastened to his leg. He tried hard to be careful, to do his job in a very normal way so he wouldn't attract attention, but it wasn't easy. Actually, he had never been the sort of man who attracted much attention, which had sometimes bothered him, but it was definitely an advantage now.

Which was all very well, but it didn't make the time go faster.

At 3:10 p.m., his shift was finally over.

Now for the last step—the most dangerous part of all. He told himself once again to do this step just like he'd done everything else that day: no muss, no fuss. Stay calm. Take it easy. You can do this.

Changing back into his street clothes in the locker room, he didn't put his work pants into his locker as usual. Instead, he rolled them up and tucked them under his arm. Then he headed for the storage room where his treasure awaited him.

The room was still empty. There was no sign that anything had been disturbed. Landis was almost afraid to look under the platform. He shoved his hand under it gingerly. Nothing. He pushed his hand farther. Still nothing. What on earth?! Then his fingers touched rough paper. Ah! He had pushed the bags in farther than he remembered. He told himself sternly to stop this fussing. It was going well. It would keep going well if he just stayed calm.

His plan was to arrange the money in the bottom of the bag and his pants on top, so it would look as if he were simply taking his work clothes home to be washed. He did that every couple of weeks. Most of his co-workers did that, too, and the guards were used to it.

But when Landis had stuffed all the money into his bag, there was no room at the top for his pants. He hadn't realized how much room 8,000 banknotes would take when they weren't compressed between wooden blocks.

He dumped out the money and began again, stacking the bills more efficiently, trying to compress them a little between the sides of the bag. But that just made the bag look suspiciously full—too full for just a shirt and a pair of pants. He dumped everything on the floor a third time and this time he only filled the bag with enough money to make it look normal. That was good—but it left almost a quarter of the banknotes lying on the floor.

Landis swore under his breath. What to do?

He supposed the only thing to do was to push the remaining money back under the platform and try his bag trick a second time, a couple of weeks later.

The problem was that he might not have an extra couple of weeks. Landis's plan was really only good enough to cover him for a short while—three or four weeks at the most. His fake money bricks would obviously be discovered sooner or later. All his efforts with the regulation packaging and the extra date stamps had simply been to make his bricks undetectable until someone broke them open at a Federal Reserve bank in some other part of the country. By that time, so many people would have handled the bricks that it would be almost impossible to establish who was to blame. That was the essence of Landis's plan.

Once discovered, of course, the serial numbers of the stolen bills would be broadcast all over the country, and any bills that Landis hadn't already exchanged would become worthless. So it was important to exchange as much of the money as possible in the shortest possible time. Waiting two weeks to bring out the rest of the money risked losing it altogether.

On the other hand, what were the alternatives?

Landis tried to think, but it became too confusing. This wasn't the time or place. Better to get most of the money out now and figure out the rest later. It was getting late; his co-workers were leaving and he was losing the advantage of joining the crowd.

He hastily pushed the rest of the money back under the platform and stood up. Shoving his work pants in on top of the bag, he clamped it under his arm and headed for the building's front entrance.

The corridor ahead of him slowly filled with people at shift's end. By the time he approached the gate, he was one of several dozen co-workers eager to get home. Landis tried hard to put himself firmly in that same frame of mind. This was just an ordinary day, and he was glad to be finished with work and going home. Just an ordinary day. That was the thing to remember: an ordinary day. Nothing special going on. Work was over, and a hot eggnog was waiting for him in front of his living room fireplace.

Just before the gate he came within range of the guard's roving eyes. The guard saw the bag right away. He frowned and raised his eyebrows questioningly. Landis smiled and pulled out a pantleg, holding it toward the guard, but he kept walking. He saw the uncertainty in the guard's eyes, a brief hesitation. All packages were supposed to be inspected, but in practice it was left to a guard's discretion.

The moment passed, and Landis was out through the gate.

ONCE HE WAS SAFELY HOME with the loot and his excitement had died down a little, Landis's most immediate challenge was how to dispose of it.

The $20 bills all had to be changed—either into smaller or larger bills. This couldn't be done at any bank since they kept records, and anyway, they'd be the first to be notified by the Bureau. No, Landis decided, the bills would have to be changed by making hundreds of very small purchases, each paid for with a brand new $20 bill.

As he did the calculations, Landis realized with a shock that he really hadn't thought through this part of the operation very carefully. Disposing of these bills wouldn't merely involve hundreds of purchases, it would be thousands—8,000 once he'd gotten out the other banknotes in the storeroom. How many purchases could you make in an ordinary day—five, six? And if you really cranked up the pace, maybe 10...15...20?

Even at 20 purchases a day, it would take him...Landis scribbled busily...400 days to exchange all that money!

Landis sat on his sofa in his living room with his pen and his scribbler, looking at the numbers. He felt a little stunned. How on earth was he going to manage this?

Obviously, he would have to involve other people.

The next day, Landis called in two friends—Charlie Nelson and William Giles—and two cousins, Roger Patterson and Edith

Chase. When he showed them the money, they were utterly amazed. Charlie Nelson smacked himself on the forehead and danced around like a demented monkey. "Holy smokes!" he kept marveling. "Holy smokes!" Edith had to threaten to throw a pot of water over him to calm him down.

The group worked out a plan to fan out across the nearby Prince Georges county, each making at least a dozen small purchases every day. The actual purchases would be each person's reward; the change from each purchase would be returned to Landis.

It sounded good, and Landis celebrated the New Year happily. Yes, indeed, his new life was sure going to be great! New clothes, a new car—maybe a brand-new Mercury with a hydramatic transmission and fat whitewalls. A fur coat for his wife. New bikes for his sons—the kind with gears.

But after only a few more days, it became clear that the plan wasn't perfect. Or perhaps one should say that it was perfect for his friends, but not so perfect for Landis. His friends were spending his money as fast as they could, but the "change" from their purchases didn't seem to be amounting to much. More and more of their purchases weren't small at all. Roger Patterson even phoned to ask whether he could use some of the money to pay some debts. Landis reluctantly said all right, go ahead, you can use "a few bills"—and Patterson went ahead and used $6,000 to pay down a gambling debt from which there was no change at all!

Things went from bad to worse. Merchants began calling the Prince Georges County police to report that certain persons seemed to have embarked on a spending spree that was knocking everyone's socks off. They were buying astonishing amounts of liquor, clothes, appliances, and groceries, and paying for everything with spanking new $20 bills. Edith Chase had bought an entire living room suite that way. A bartender called in to say that Charlie Nelson had even taken to lighting his cigars with $20 bills. What was going on here? Had somebody robbed a bank?

The police, suspecting a counterfeit ring, called in the FBI. The FBI called in the US Secret Service. Soon half a dozen agents were snooping around Prince Georges county, examining banknotes and interviewing merchants.

And then, far sooner than Landis had ever suspected, the Bureau discovered his fake money bricks.

They were discovered before they even left the Vault. As bad luck would have it, a Bureau employee happened to pick up one of the fake bricks with one hand and an authentic one with the other. He immediately noticed a difference in weight between the two. (Since Landis had no high-powered compression machine at home, he'd had to compress his fake bricks with an ordinary woodworking clamp—and since he couldn't exceed the dimensions of an authentic brick, this meant he'd only been able to squeeze approximately 3,000 banknote-sized handbills between his wooden blocks instead of the usual 4,000 banknotes. The difference in weight was significant.)

The employee immediately notified his supervisor, and the brick was broken open. When the fraud was discovered, all the other bricks in the Vault were checked as well. It didn't take them long to find the second fake brick.

When the Bureau contacted the Secret Service, the agency had already received reports of the extravagant spending going on in Prince Georges county. It didn't take a genius to make the connection. The agents closed in and began making arrests. Within two days, Landis and his four cohorts were behind bars.

Everyone confessed—including Landis's "friend" Charlie

Nelson, who admitted that he'd planned to steal everyone's money once the banknote-exchange had been completed! "When those thieves got through stealing from each other," he said, "I was gonna take it all."

Landis (who was wearing a flashy new cashmere overcoat when he was arrested) gave up and led authorities to the unused storeroom where police found $32,000 still hidden under the platform. Of the other $128,000, they managed to recover $95,000, plus a grand total of $6,000 in small bills—the amount that his friends were going to "give back" to Landis after their purchases.

For his part in the heist, Landis received three to nine years in prison. Charlie, Roger, and William got lesser sentences, ranging from 20 months to three years.

And Edith Chase? Well, even though women in the United States had finally gotten the vote in 1920 and judges had had over 30 years to get used to the idea of gender equality, some were still having trouble with the concept. So, even though it was 1954, the judge in this case decided that since Edith was a woman, she couldn't really be held as responsible for her actions as the men. She was merely placed on probation.

The Napoleon of Crime

JUST AFTER MIDNIGHT on May 14, 1876, three men in top hats and tails stood at the corner of Piccadilly and Old Bond Street in London, England. A low fog swirled around them, chilly and damp. At this hour, the shops, the sidewalks, and even the streets were deserted. The gas flames in the streetlamps flickered restlessly in the mist.

The three men spoke briefly, then headed down Old Bond Street. Several blocks along, one of them ducked into an angled doorway that allowed him a clear view of the street ahead. The other two stopped a few steps later in front of an art gallery emblazoned with the sign Thomas Agnew & Sons. The gallery's front windows were filled with paintings of various subjects and sizes, but the two men seemed most interested in a smaller window on the gallery's second story, directly above.

After a last look in all directions, one of the two men—a barrel-chested giant with mutton-chop whiskers—clasped his hands into a stirrup and bent down. His short companion, a dapper gentleman dressed in an expensive frock coat, placed his right foot into the giant's hands and gripped his shoulders. With a single well-practiced heave, the giant hurled the little man up onto the gallery's overhanging roof, enabling him to grasp the second-story window ledge.

A few quick wrenches with a small crowbar and the window popped open. The little man disappeared inside. Down below in the street, his assistant disappeared just as quickly.

Inside the gallery, the burglar found himself in an unfurnished, unlit room. Three of its walls were bare, but on the fourth wall, dimly lit by light that filtered in from the streetlamps, he immediately saw what he was looking for.

Georgiana, Duchess of Devonshire.

The portrait, painted by the great English artist Thomas Gainsborough, had recently been bought by the gallery for over 10,000 pounds sterling—the highest price ever paid for a painting in the history of art. The purchase had made headlines all over the western world.

She looked down at him from her gilt frame with an almost mocking smile—imperious yet beckoning, irresistible. "The most exquisite beauty that ever graced a canvas" one art critic had raved. Her ample curls cascaded down onto her shoulders under an enormous plumed hat.

The burglar stared, transfixed.

After a while, he realized he was listening to the steady, rhythmic snoring of a night watchman downstairs who was supposed to be guarding this treasure.

There was no time to waste. The burglar felt around in his coat and pulled out a sharp knife and a small pot of paste. Lifting the portrait off the wall, he carefully cut the canvas out of its frame, then smeared the paste evenly across its back to make it more flexible. Then he rolled it up very carefully with the painted side outwards, to avoid cracking the surface, and slipped it inside his coat. He stuck his head out of the window and gave a low whistle.

He heard a low whistle in return.

A few seconds later, he scrambled off the roof, falling into the waiting arms of his giant assistant. The third man suddenly appeared out of his doorway. The three men continued on their way down Old Bond Street, chatting nonchalantly as if nothing had happened.

NEWS OF THE THEFT of the *Duchess* caused a huge uproar, both in the world of art and that of crime. Scotland Yard, Britain's national police headquarters, immediately sent its agents scurrying all over England, trying to pick up the missing portrait's trail. When the agents returned empty-handed, circulars and photos of the painting were sent to police forces all over the world. Advertisements were placed in many European newspapers and magazines, and a huge reward was offered for the painting's safe return. The Pinkerton Agency, America's largest private detective agency, was engaged to investigate rumors that the painting might have been stolen for one of America's steel or oil barons. Many of them had large art collections.

In fact, the little man who had stolen the Gainsborough portrait was Adam Worth, one of the most successful thieves of modern times. In the criminal underworld, Worth was known as "The Napoleon of Crime"—both because of his success and his small size. He was an American who had recently moved his criminal operations to England, where he had bought a racing stable, a large steam yacht (*The Shamrock*), and a stately mansion in Piccadilly, where he entertained many of the bankers and barons he regularly fleeced.

As crooks went, Worth was definitely a cut above average. He was charming and gracious. He was disciplined, loyal, and a workaholic. He didn't drink, fight, or boast. He used his brains instead of his muscles, and was generous to a fault. Anyone working for Adam Worth knew that Worth would spend his last nickel to help them out if they got into legal trouble.

Worth was the son of a German tailor who had emigrated to the United States in 1849, when Worth was just five years old. Watching their parents struggling desperately to scrape together a living year after year apparently convinced all three of the couple's children—Adam, a younger brother John, and a sister named Harriet—that trying to make an honest living in 1840s America was a hopeless proposition. Ashamed of their poverty and impatient for the good life that the family had hoped to achieve by emigrating, all three joined the world of crime—the two boys as thieves, and the daughter as wife of a dishonest lawyer. Only Adam turned out to have a real knack for it.

By the time Worth stole the *Duchess*, he had been a professional thief for almost 20 years. He had stolen jewels, banknotes, and other valuables worth millions, but had never once been convicted of a criminal offence. Both Scotland Yard and the Pinkerton Agency knew all about him and had already spent untold man-hours trying to outwit him, but Worth had always been too clever for them.

But now something quite unexpected happened.

Adam Worth, a man who had always kept control of his emotions and had never cared a fig about art (except for its value as loot), became utterly fascinated by the *Duchess*.

As he studied her portrait more carefully during the days after the theft, he became so drawn to her that he decided to keep her.

This did not please his two partners in crime. The three men had agreed to steal the portrait, sell it back to the gallery for its pawn value (usually 25 percent of its retail price), then split the proceeds three ways. Since their theft of the *Duchess* had caused even more uproar in the art world than her recent purchase by the Thomas Agnew gallery—thus pushing her value even higher—the two men had been expecting very large payouts.

Worth did eventually pay the two men their shares, but the amount was far less than they believed they were owed. Their partnership broke up in anger, with the two men vowing revenge. It was a vow that would cost Adam Worth dearly one day.

BUT IN THE MEANTIME, as he continued his career of robbing banks and stealing millions, Worth's infatuation with the *Duchess* continued to grow. It wasn't long before just gazing at her now and then, in the secret little gallery he had built for her in his London mansion, wasn't enough.

He had a special false-bottomed trunk constructed so he could take her along on his many voyages. He even had a leather-maker build him a false-bottomed briefcase, so that during the day, as he went about his business, she was rarely more than an arm's length away. At night, in hotel rooms, he took her out and set her up on a table or counter so he could gaze on her to his heart's content.

As rumors about Worth and the *Duchess* began to spread through the underworld, some of his friends suspected that his infatuation with the painting stemmed from the fact that the *Duchess* looked surprisingly like Kitty Flynn. Kitty was an Irish barmaid who'd had a long affair (and two daughters) with Worth in the early 1870s. They were still friends, but in 1874 Kitty had left Worth and emigrated to the United States, where she'd married a rich Cuban playboy. People close to Adam Worth claimed that he had never gotten over Kitty's rejection.

Perhaps. Perhaps not. Adam Worth wasn't in the habit of telling people his innermost feelings. To be a successful thief, you had to keep your eyes open and your mouth shut, and Worth was very good at that. It made him a good listener and something of a mystery man at the same time.

ONE MAN WHO FOUND THE RUMORS about Adam Worth and the *Duchess* extremely intriguing was William Pinkerton of the Pinkerton Detective Agency. Nicknamed "The Eye," Pinkerton was a world-famous detective, street-smart and ruthless. He had caught and brought to justice more famous crooks than any other man alive. His list of captures included Jesse James, Butch Cassidy and Harry Longabaugh (from "The Wild Bunch"), Kid Curry, "Texas Jack" Searcy, and Maximilian Shinburn. He had every intention of adding Adam Worth to that list.

The two men had met on a number of social occasions and, to everyone's surprise, they'd liked each other immediately. Even though Worth was a criminal, Pinkerton found him to be smart, resourceful, and courageous. He also liked the fact that Worth never used a gun when committing his crimes. Worth, for his part, admired Pinkerton's brilliant detective work. He was impressed by the way Pinkerton never gave up, and that he always fought fair.

Whenever they met in a bar or restaurant in London, Paris, or New York, they bought each other drinks and spent an hour or two chatting. At the same time, there was never any doubt in either man's mind about what was going on. Pinkerton was determined to put Worth in jail, and Worth was determined not to let Pinkerton succeed. It was an ongoing battle of wits and tactics, even though they both managed to make it look as if they were just two men having a casual conversation.

Mere months after the theft of the *Duchess*, Pinkerton's spies had already informed the detective about underworld rumors linking the theft to Adam Worth. But more definitive evidence fell into his hands almost a year later when Little Joe Elliott, one of Worth's two former partners, was arrested in New York for forging checks. In an effort to reduce his prison sentence, Elliott requested a meeting with Pinkerton and betrayed Worth, giving Pinkerton all the details.

It was, according to the law, only hearsay evidence, not enough to arrest Worth, but it confirmed Pinkerton's suspicions. (And a few months later, the other partner, giant Jack "Junka" Phillips, gave a similar story to Scotland Yard.)

As public frustration over the loss of the *Duchess* grew and pressure on the police to find her increased, Scotland Yard appealed to the Pinkerton Agency for help. Pinkerton agreed. During his next trip to the United States, only hours after Worth had checked out of New York's Astor House Hotel, Pinkerton's detectives raided the place, looking for Worth and the painting. Only days after that, one of Pinkerton's men tracked Worth down to a fancy hotel in Buffalo, New York, where he was having dinner with his sister and brother-in-law. The detective waited until he saw Worth coming through the lobby with his briefcase under his arm, then gave chase. Racing out of the lobby, Worth almost ran into the arms of two other detectives, who grabbed at him but missed.

Worth hastily took the next train out of town, and for the remainder of his travels in America—which he shortened considerably—he kept the *Duchess* safely hidden in a Boston warehouse.

But if Worth had expected to find peace and tranquility on his return to London, he was mistaken. When he got back, he found that his mansion had been raided and a Scotland Yard detective permanently stationed out front!

Clearly, it was time to take a very long holiday.

Worth spent the next several years traveling throughout the Middle East, Europe, and South Africa. He robbed mail trains, hijacked diamond shipments, fleeced banks, and raided safety deposit boxes. He swindled investment houses, stole bonds, faked insurance claims, and blew up safes. And whenever he could, he took the *Duchess* with him. Where once he had merely hidden her in a traveling trunk or carried her around in a briefcase, he now kept her rolled up and tucked into the inside pocket of his overcoat. And at night, after he had gazed his fill, he sandwiched her between two smoothly sanded pine boards and hid her under his mattress.

As the years went by and Worth managed to evade every effort by both William Pinkerton and Scotland Yard to recover the *Duchess*, the heat finally did die down. Worth returned to his London mansion, his racing stable, and his thoroughbreds. Scotland Yard eventually withdrew the lookout in front of his house. Worth became the mentor for a whole new generation of criminals, who worked for him and with him. He even got married at some point along the way, and had a son and daughter with his wife.

But through it all—despite threats from Scotland Yard, blackmail attempts by other criminals, and even enticing offers from insurance companies—he continued to refuse all attempts to convince or to coerce him to give up the *Duchess*.

AND THEN, IN 1892, 16 years after the theft, Adam Worth made the mistake that every police force in the western world had been hoping for.

It had actually begun in February of 1884 with the news that an old friend and partner, Charlie Bullard, had been caught trying to rob a bank in Liège, Belgium. Bullard was sentenced to 12 years' hard labor in the Prison de Louvain.

Prisons in Belgium were notorious for their brutality. Sentences longer than five years were considered death sentences. Few inmates were able to survive in Belgian prisons for longer than that.

For the next eight years, Adam Worth tried everything he could think of to free his old partner. He paid bribes. He hired expensive lawyers. He petitioned politicians with clemency requests. Nothing worked.

Finally, in 1892 Worth decided to travel to Belgium himself. The reasons he gave to his wife and his associates were vague, but he was probably planning to organize a team to break into the Prison de Louvain to free Bullard by force.

When he arrived in Liège, however, he discovered he was too late. Charlie Bullard had died.

The news hit Worth hard. He spent the next several days just walking around Liège, mourning the loss of his old friend.

As he walked, Worth couldn't help noticing that the armored express van that made daily currency deliveries to the city's banks was guarded only by a single armed driver and an unarmed apprentice. Intrigued, even though his thoughts were distracted by Bullard's death, Worth followed the van. He saw that occasionally, when they had deliveries for several adjacent buildings, the two men made their deliveries simultaneously, leaving the van briefly unguarded.

Death or no death, it seemed too good an opportunity to waste. Charlie Bullard would have understood.

Worth sent off two quick telegrams, asking Johnny Curtin, an American bank robber hiding out in London, and Big Dutch Alonzo, a London mobster, to join him.

When the men arrived, Worth laid out the plan. He would arrange to have a delivery sent by the armored express van to an office close to one of Liège's downtown banks. The driver would presumably do the bank delivery, while the apprentice delivered Worth's bogus package. As soon as the van was unattended, Worth would slip inside, smash the lock off its strongbox, scoop its contents into a canvas bag, and hand it off to Curtin, who would be passing by as an innocent tourist. Big Dutch Alonzo would hover in the vicinity, ready to apply some muscle if anything went wrong.

Simple, quick, and easy.

For years afterwards, people wondered whether Curtin and Alonzo were somehow in league with Worth's former partners who had sworn revenge on him. Because what happened during the heist two days later was hard to understand any other way.

It began exactly as planned. At 9:30 that morning, the van drew up beside the bank at 31 Boulevard Frère Orban, right next to the café in which the three men were waiting. The driver filled a money sack from his strongbox and replaced its lock. As he left the van and headed for the bank, his apprentice sprinted away up a side street with a box.

Within seconds, Worth was in the van with his canvas bag. A quick, practiced blow and the strongbox lock was lying on the floor mat. Twenty seconds later, its entire contents had been stuffed into Worth's bag and Worth was handing it out through the van door to Curtin, who should have been passing by at that instant.

But Curtin wasn't there.

Dumbfounded, Worth stuck his head out the door and looked around. There was Curtin, rushing away *in the opposite direction!*

Worth looked around frantically for Alonzo. He too was just disappearing down a nearby sidestreet.

What in tarnation was going on?

There was no time to speculate. Clutching the bag, Worth jumped out of the van and began to hurry away himself.

"Stop thief! Stop thief!" someone shouted.

Worth looked in the direction of the voice. A man in a railway uniform was pointing at him excitedly. "Stop him!"

At this point, the returning van driver caught sight of Worth and gave chase. So did the man in the railway uniform. The three men raced down the boulevard, Adam Worth drawing steadily ahead. For a few moments, it looked as if Worth would be able to outrace his pursuers.

But at the rue Saint-Veronique, a young police patrolman heard the shouts and sprang into action. A block later, Worth could hear the patrolman's footsteps pounding away a short distance behind. In desperation, he flung his bag into a nearby alley and tried to dodge into the shopping crowds. Too late! He was tackled by several citizens and went down. The young policemen leaped on top of him and clapped him into handcuffs.

It was game over for Adam Worth.

Or was it?

Worth told the police his name was Edward Grey. Then he clammed up tight. Despite days of interrogation, he refused to say anything more—and despite their betrayal, he even refused to rat on his accomplices.

For a while, it looked as if the prosecution would have to be satisfied with charging "Edward Grey" with simple snatch-and-grab thievery—resulting in only a brief stint in prison or even just a fine.

Frustrated, the police tried one last tactic. They sent Worth's photograph and description to police forces all over Europe and North America.

That did it.

A chorus of replies informed the Belgian police that they had succeeded in catching Adam Worth, one of the greatest thieves of all time.

Armed with this new evidence, the Belgian Court now confidently charged Adam Worth with being a professional thief who had planned and carried out the carefully organized robbery of an official Belgian armored delivery van. After several days of testimony, the jury took only minutes to agree. Worth was sentenced to seven years of solitary confinement with hard labor in the Prison de Louvain—the very prison he had probably come to Belgium to attack.

It wasn't long before the effects of the Belgian prison system on Adam Worth began to show. He sank into a deep depression. Then he developed bronchitis. The prison doctor at de Louvain treated this with a crude surgical operation on the inside of Worth's nose, which led to frequent, violent nosebleeds and crippling headaches.

As news of Worth's condition spread, he began to receive offers from lawyers, politicians, and even police representatives to hand over the *Duchess* in return for a shortened prison sentence.

But Worth refused.

Then Worth discovered that Johnny Curtin's betrayal had not stopped with his cowardly disappearance on the Boulevard Frère Orban. Curtin had fled back to England and presented himself to Worth's wife as her savior. It wasn't long before he had convinced the distraught woman to sign over all of Worth's possessions—his mansion, his yacht, his racing stables. Then Curtin staged what amounted to England's biggest garage sale, selling everything and leaving Worth's wife penniless. Shortly afterward, he disappeared.

When word of Curtin's treachery reached Worth, he gripped his prison bars with both fists and bellowed like a wounded bull. But he still adamantly refused to hand over the *Duchess*.

A year later, word arrived from America that Kitty Flynn, the great love of his life, had died in New York of a kidney disease.

Worth closed his eyes in pain, but held on.

He kept holding on even when he was informed that his wife had gone mad and, being penniless, had been put into a London lunatic asylum.

Worth was now at rock bottom. His wife was insane, the love of his life was dead, his horses, houses, yacht, and reputation were gone, his health ruined. All he had left was the *Duchess*, wrapped in a cocoon of pure silk in a Brooklyn warehouse where he had hidden her before heading for Belgium.

WHEN THE BELGIAN PRISON AUTHORITIES finally released Adam Worth in 1897, two years early for good behavior, the man who had once been the Napoleon of Crime was a broken man. He was dying of tuberculosis, and filled with regret. With his wife as good as dead, he decided the only thing left to do before his own death was to try to provide some security for his son and daughter.

Thus, it wasn't long before William Pinkerton received a telegram at his Agency office in Chicago: *Letter awaiting you at house; send for it. Signed, Roy.*

Pinkerton immediately called home. His daughter informed

him that a strange man had called and left a letter, stating that it was important.

It was. The writer—who was clearly Adam Worth—wished to inform Pinkerton that he was finally prepared to open negotiations for the return of the *Duchess*.

The two men met in Pinkerton's office two days later. It was a meeting of historic importance for both: the western world's most famous thief and the western world's most famous detective, both having spent almost a lifetime trying to outwit each other. Worth was a wanted man in America; Pinkerton could have arrested him on the spot. But they were past that now. Their battle was over.

Worth opened negotiations by demanding $25,000 in cash, plus immunity from prosecution. He promised that the money would only be used for the support and education of his children. Pinkerton agreed, but insisted that the deal had to be handled in such a way that he—the American symbol of justice and crime-busting—couldn't be seen as an accomplice to a crime.

So the two men cooked up a story in which the relentless William Pinkerton, after years of heroic effort, had finally tracked down the famous *Duchess* to an undisclosed location in the American Midwest. But the current holder of the painting turned out not to be the thief. The current holder had been given the painting by a man—presumably the actual thief—shortly before the thief had died. So the true thief was dead, and the current holder was now claiming the posted reward for the painting's return.

Once they agreed on the story, the two men shook on it. Then Adam Worth pulled the rolled-up *Duchess* carefully out of the inside pocket of his overcoat and solemnly handed her over to William Pinkerton.

The newspapers of the day bought the story completely.

For William Pinkerton, the return of the *Duchess* became his career's crowning glory and his greatest accomplishment. Adam Worth, on the other hand, could now face his imminent death with peace of mind. Pinkerton had promised to keep an eye on his children and to ensure that they were not cheated out of their support money.

Pinkerton kept his promise. When Worth died on January 8, 1902 in Camden, England, his children were with him, safe and secure. In fact, due in large part to Pinkerton's efforts, they weren't even aware that their father had been a famous thief.

Pinkerton kept an eye on Worth's children for many years after their father's death. He gave them fatherly advice, which they may have heeded, because neither of them followed in their father's footsteps.

The daughter, by some accounts, looked surprisingly like the *Duchess* at an early age. And the son—in this story's most ironic twist—eventually joined the Pinkerton Agency and became one of its most accomplished detectives!

Banknotes from Heaven

ON JULY 19, 1949, at 2:50 p.m.—just before closing time—two bandits entered the Imperial Bank of Canada in the prosperous little gold-mining town of Larder Lake in northern Ontario. The bank was one of half a dozen two-storied, false-fronted businesses lining Larder Lake's muddy main street. A row of mostly black automobiles stood parked right up against the buildings' fronts—Larder Lake had never had much patience with city-slicker features like sidewalks.

The bandits—Victor Desmarais and Leo Martial—hailed from Montreal, Canada's undisputed bank robbery capital. In the 1940s, bandits were robbing Montreal's banks at the rate of one every 93 minutes, and competition was becoming fierce. So when they read newspaper accounts of the gold-mining boom in Ontario's northland, Desmarais and Martial decided to take a break from the city and give the country a try. After all, where there was lots of gold, there was bound to be lots of cash. The plan started looking even better when they discovered that Larder Lake only had one bank. This had all the advantages of one-stop shopping.

Best of all, the town had a seaplane base on the lake nearby. They could travel to Larder Lake by train, then fly out of town with their loot by chartered float-plane.

The setup couldn't have been more perfect.

The bandits arrived in town wearing the only disguise that

made any sense in a place like Larder Lake: ordinary work clothes. Each carried a suitcase with some tools and a revolver inside. Normally, they would have hidden their revolvers in their jackets, but they couldn't wear any—it was July and Larder Lake was roasting. It was also buzzing with deerflies.

There were no other customers when they entered the bank. A paddle fan turned lazily just below the high ceiling, but it hadn't made the place much cooler. Two tellers were doing paperwork behind the grilles of old-fashioned teller's cages. Both women looked up expectantly.

"This is a holdup!" Desmarais announced, waving his gun. Martial waved his gun, too. The tellers were amazed. There had never been a bank holdup in Larder Lake before.

"Where's the manager?" Martial demanded.

The tellers didn't know. Manager Albert Gary often spent time away from his desk without explaining where he was going.

Desmarais looked annoyed. He asked them whether either of them knew the combination to the vault.

They didn't.

Martial slapped at a deerfly and swore under his breath. Desmarais decided they'd have to drill into the vault. There wasn't time to wait until the manager got back.

"The vault's open," the first teller said.

"Wouldn't he come back before closing time?" Martial asked.

"The vault's open," the teller repeated. "It's never locked during the day."

The bandits were astounded. Was this really how people did business in the boonies? They quickly herded both tellers to the back of the bank where the vault was located and checked.

It was true. The vault door was wide open. They might as well have hung a "Help Yourself" sign on it!

Desmarais kept guard over the tellers while Martial quickly stuffed all the money he could find in the vault—about $15,000—into their two suitcases. At this moment the bell over the front door jangled.

The bandits froze.

"Front door's not locked yet," one of the tellers said. She moved around a corner and looked. "Gerry Hamson," she said. "He's a mining inspector."

"Anybody home?" boomed a loud voice. "Hey, where is everybody?"

"Right back here," Martial said, stepping around the corner with his revolver raised. "Don't move, or I'll shoot."

It was by now 3:05 p.m.

"Lock the front door and bring him in here," Martial said to the first teller, indicating the astonished inspector. "I want everyone in the vault."

When everyone was seated on overturned footlockers in the vault, Desmarais proceeded to tie up the inspector, who looked as if he might cause trouble. "I don't want any of you to start yelling for at least half an hour," Desmarais ordered. "What's the name of a taxi company in this town?"

The inspector maintained an angry silence. After a long pause the second teller said, "There's only Toni Gervanni."

"Gervanni? All right, call him up. Tell him to come to the back of the bank for a parcel."

While the teller unhooked the earpiece and cranked the handle on the bank's only phone, Martial hauled the two suitcases to the back door. Then he hustled the second teller into the vault. When the taxi arrived five minutes later, the three hostages were securely locked in the vault and the bandits were waiting outside the bank, suitcases bulging.

"Take us to the seaplane base," Desmarais said. "Leavern Brothers Air Service."

Gervanni explained that he had to pick up a parcel first, but that after he'd done that, he would take them to the base.

The bandits wrenched open the car's rear doors, flung in their suitcases, and slid in after them. "You're going to take us to the seaplane base right now," Desmerais growled, shoving his revolver against the back of Gervanni's head. "Never mind about the parcel."

Gervanni began to shake. The taxi moved off in a series of jackrabbit lurches. Desmerais smacked the revolver against Gervanni's neck and ordered him to settle down. That didn't improve Gervanni's driving.

The floatplane base was 18 miles (28 km) out of town, and the bandits arrived there at 3:45 p.m. They had ordered a seaplane to fly them out to Val D'Or, a small city in northern Quebec several hundred miles to the east. Val D'Or had an airport that offered a daily commercial flight south to Montreal.

They told Gervanni to wait in front of Leavern Brothers' tiny shack of an office while they checked the arrangements. Bush pilot Jack Lamont was already there, peering curiously through the front window as they drove up. After a short discussion, Desmarais waved Gervanni away. The frightened taxi driver drove off in a spray of gravel.

What happened next is a matter of some dispute. Some reports claim that Jack Lamont had caught sight of Desmarais' revolver as he climbed out of the taxi, and so the fact that his floatplane wouldn't start was actually a trick. Some say Lamont just got lucky. Whatever the case, when the suitcases had been stowed and the bandits seated in Lamont's little single-engine Aeronca, the motor churned and churned but wouldn't catch. Lamont fussed with various dials and knobs and kept adjusting the throttle, but nothing worked. Finally the bandits lost patience.

"Haven't you guys got another plane?" Martial demanded.

Lamont shook his head. He said he couldn't figure out what was wrong; the plane had worked just fine yesterday. He offered to phone around to see if any of the owners of the other floatplanes moored at the base might be willing to take over the job. He disappeared into his office to start phoning.

After a further 10 minutes, the bandits became alarmed. Lamont seemed to be spending an awfully long time on the phone. Desmarais started checking out other planes tied to the dock and found one with its keys dangling in the ignition. "Get that pilot!" he shouted to Martial. "He can fly us out with this one."

Martial ran off to bring back the pilot, but returned almost immediately to report that Lamont had disappeared. There was no one in the office.

Desmarais swore a volley of oaths. He had let Gervanni drive off because he'd expected to be in the air minutes later. It was almost certain that the taxi driver had by now alerted the police.

Their only hope was that plane.

Although neither man was a pilot, both had flown in floatplanes before. They had also watched Lamont trying to start his Aeronca. It wasn't much, but it was their only chance. There was no more time to lose.

They hauled their suitcases into the new plane, threw off the tie lines, and leaped inside. Desmarais took over the pilot's seat and turned the key. The dashboard lit up and hummed. He pushed the starter. The engine began to whine. He pulled on the throttle and the engine sprang into life. He shouted something at Martial, who couldn't hear him over the noise. The plane began to move.

Desmarais pulled on the throttle some more and the plane gathered speed. It was now heading toward a boat moored just offshore, and Desmarais searched frantically for the rudder. Once he found it, it didn't take him long to figure out how it worked. The plane straightened sharply and headed out into the lake.

Desmarais shouted something that sounded like "hold on!" and pulled the throttle out as far as it would go. The engine howl turned into a roar and the plane sped up quickly. Now they were leaving a rooster tail of foam in their wake. They plowed across the lake at full power, all the way to the other side—but the plane wouldn't lift off. They turned around and tried it again in the opposite direction. Still no luck.

By now, the shore was coming alive with rubberneckers. Toni Gervanni had indeed called Ralph Paul (whose rather grand title of "police chief" hid the fact that he was actually Larder Lake's only policeman) as soon as he'd gotten back to town. So had Jack Lamont. The hostages had been found and freed, and word of the robbery had spread through the town like wildfire. Ralph Paul had quickly called up the only policeman in nearby Virginiatown, Constable Lloyd Westlake, and the two men were assembling a posse of townspeople to give chase.

Up at the lake, half the town was now watching the plane buzzing frantically back and forth across the water like a berserk mosquito. It still could not lift off. Some people were yelling, some waving; some cheered and some booed. Larder Lake hadn't had so much excitement in years!

Finally, Desmarais tried pulling back on the stick, and that did it! The plane reared abruptly into the air—but as it did, it also began banking to the left, which slowed its rise. Roaring at full throttle, it swung back toward the dock at a height of perhaps 30 feet (10 m), sending people stampeding frantically in all directions.

With Desmarais desperately trying to synchronize the controls, the plane swerved right and then left, each turn frustrating his efforts to get its nose up high enough to clear the approaching trees. It was too late now to try to turn around—the plane was heading straight for a slot in the trees just west of the parking lot.

And then it *almost* made it through the slot—but not quite. A wing tip touched a tree and then a float caught a snag, and the plane spun around and tore into a thicket of evergreens that seemed to grab at it with a hundred branches. The plane was thrown sideways and then it flipped over, breaking limbs and snapping treetops as it began to fall. It sounded oddly like rifle shots going off at a shooting gallery.

At this point, its passenger door broke open, revealing an upside-down Martial frantically clutching at a torn or unhooked safety belt. The suitcases had also come loose and were flinging about in the back of the plane. Then they both flew out the open door.

Moments later, an explosion of banknotes scattered like confetti over the bush land bordering Larder Lake. It startled several trappers who were working their trap lines near the lake that day, and thrilled the town residents who came scrambling over from the floatplane base. Some of the money was gathered up by the posse, and some was turned in by onlookers, but some was never recovered. As one Larder Lake resident put it wryly, payday came early for some of Larder Lake's citizens that day.

Miraculously, the plane didn't catch fire when it finally smacked down in a patch of dense underbrush a short distance from the base. The two bandits survived the crash with only cuts and bruises. They promptly disappeared into the bush, with Ralph Paul's posse—by then numbering over a hundred men—in hot pursuit.

Leo Martial didn't get very far. He was captured just over an hour later, at gunpoint, on Highway 66. He had followed a trap line that seemed to be headed away from town, but its direction had changed and he hadn't noticed. He ran right into the arms of some of Ralph Paul's volunteers who had been searching the bush around the lakeshore.

Victor Desmarais, however, managed to avoid capture until about 1:30 the next morning. He stayed clear of the trails, working his way deeper and deeper into the bush. Whether he eventually became lost or whether he decided to jump a passing freight train is unclear, but by morning he had returned to the rail line that ran along the edge of town. He was finally caught and arrested in the vicinity of the Larder Lake station, where two small boys saw him and reported him to the posse. He was hungry, badly fly-bitten, and totally exhausted.

Justice in the 1940s was handed out a lot more quickly than it is today. A mere two weeks later, both thieves had been arraigned, tried, and sentenced, and were already on their way to the Kingston Penitentiary. Charged with illegal confinement, possession of a prohibited weapon, and armed robbery, they had been sentenced to seven years each.

The feeling around Larder Lake was that if they'd also been charged with the gross stupidity of their getaway attempt, the length of their sentences might have been much greater.

Meanwhile, the Larder Lake robbery brought the town a degree of notoriety it could well have done without. Just over a decade later, it became the target of another major heist, this one a load of gold bullion being transferred to Toronto from the surrounding gold mines. Once again a plane was used, but this time it was operated by a real pilot. The thieves in this caper were never caught.

The Classiest Thief in Manhattan

IN THE 1920S, Manhattan's classiest hotel was without doubt The Plaza, located on the corner of Fifth Avenue and Central Park South. Its luxurious suites were a home away from home for many of the world's most rich and famous. The great comedian Charlie Chaplin stayed at The Plaza when he was in town. So did novelist F. Scott Fitzgerald. Presidents and kings booked suites months in advance. Some patrons, like the fabulously wealthy Woolworth department store heiress Mrs. Jessie Woolworth Donahue and her stockbroker husband James P. Donahue, even maintained a permanent apartment at the hotel.

On September 29, 1925, the Donahues arrived at The Plaza to spend a week in New York—Mr. Donahue to see to some business matters and Mrs. Donahue to be fitted with some of the costliest pearl necklaces ever produced by Cartier of Paris. As was usual in those days, the New York newspapers reported the Donahues' arrival and the purpose of their stay in the society pages.

It was an announcement Jessie Donahue would live to regret.

Two days later, a tall, elegantly dressed man climbed out of a taxi in front of the hotel. His conservatively tailored suit, pearl-gray cravat and dignified black top hat caused the doorman to snap to instant attention. A bellhop hurried across the lobby with his hand outstretched, but the man waved him off with a casual gesture and headed for the elevator cage. "Fifth floor, my man," he ordered.

The operator bowed and closed the cage gate. "Fifth floor," he repeated obediently. The cage rose silently up the shaft and stopped, gently, five floors up. "Enjoy your stay, sir," the operator said, and bowed again. The gate slid back on well-oiled rails.

The man in the top hat waited until the elevator cage had disappeared back down the shaft. Then he headed along the richly carpeted corridor to the emergency stairway. Looking around to make sure the corridor was empty, he slipped into the stairway and climbed up to the sixth floor. Here, too, the hallway was deserted.

The Donahue apartment was only a short distance away—with a large brass 610 on the door. As he approached it, the man in the top hat drew a pair of gray silk gloves from his inside breast pocket and pulled them on. At the door, he listened intently, while watching the corridor in both directions. Then he slid a hotel pass key into the lock, gently twisted the doorknob, and pushed open the door.

Inside, he could hear female voices from somewhere deeper in the apartment. Now and then a peal of laughter. Two voices? No, three. Directly ahead of him was the empty living room, with three closed bedroom doors on the Fifth Avenue side. The master bedroom was in the middle. He knew that it had an extra-large bathroom attached to it, with its own dressing room. That's where the voices seemed to be coming from.

He moved silently across the vast expanse of living room carpet and listened again at the master bedroom door. The voices seemed to be coming from farther away, from the dressing room or the bathroom itself. Good. He turned the doorknob gingerly and eased the door open a few inches. Then a few more inches. Then enough to insert his head.

Just as he'd thought. The door between the master bedroom and its bathroom was closed. The voices were coming from behind that door.

Taking a deep breath, he slipped fully into the room. He stepped quickly to the dressing table and checked its drawers. Nothing of interest there. Then the large walnut wardrobe next to the window. Drawers, shelves—nothing he was looking for. Luggage? Just a few clothes. The bureau? Underwear in the first drawer, scarves and belts in the second. Then the third—a heavy velvet jewel box. This looked promising.

Inside was a large selection of gems—pendants, brooches, earrings. Jessie Donahue's main collection by the look of it, or at least a good portion. The lady certainly had expensive tastes. He prodded the jewels gently, letting the light from the window dance and sparkle through them.

Under a layer of linens he found more treasure—necklaces, a tiara, bracelets, chains. All high-quality, all very costly. He slipped these into his pockets, too.

But they weren't what he was looking for.

He kept rummaging.

Finally, in a leather case stuffed with tissue paper, at the very back of the drawer, he found five heavy strands of pearls.

Bingo. Five strings of pearls by Cartier, probably worth half a million dollars apiece.

If they were real.

He picked up a string and rubbed its center pearl slowly across his teeth. Back and forth. It produced a faint grating sound. A fake. Not surprising—when rich socialites ordered jewelry, they often ordered identical-looking fake sets as well, to wear in social situations where the jewels were more likely to be lost or stolen.

A burst of laughter from behind the bathroom door made him stiffen briefly. Footsteps approached. His hands hovered over the nest of pearls, ready to grab.

The footsteps stopped at the door. A metallic clank suggested that something on a hanger had been hung on a hook.

Eyes still riveted on the door, the man in the top hat slid the next string into his mouth. Another fake.

The third string produced a tiny, high-pitched squeal against his teeth. This was the real McCoy. The fourth one made the same sound. Another score. He dropped them both into his pocket.

The fifth grated.

It was time to go.

With a few practiced flicks of his hands, he straightened the linens, replaced the case, and silently closed the last drawer. Seconds later, he was back out in the corridor.

As he hurried down the stairs to the fifth floor he stripped off his gloves. At the fifth-floor elevator door, he rang the bell. The cage appeared, the operator bowed, the gate opened and closed, then sank silently down its shaft. Back in the lobby, the man nodded pleasantly to a bowing bell captain, tipped his hat at the front door to an elderly lady, and beckoned a cab. He rode the cab for a dozen blocks, got out, hailed a cab in the opposite direction, and gave the driver an Upper West Side address. There, he paid off the cab, waited until it had turned a corner, then walked another half-dozen blocks to where he really lived.

Only then did he allow himself to completely relax.

THE HEADLINE on the front page of the next day's New York *Times* trumpeted: WOOLWORTH HEIRESS ROBBED AT THE PLAZA OF $750,000 IN GEMS! THIEF ESCAPES LEAVING NO CLUE.

The article claimed that the robbery was one of the biggest on record, and included several recently purchased strings of pearls that had been insured for a million dollars alone. All the more astonishing was the fact that the theft had occurred while Mrs. Jessie Donahue had been in her bathroom immediately adjacent to the bedroom, with a maid and a masseuse in attendance the entire time.

Descriptions of the gems, provided by Cartier of Paris, were immediately broadcast all over the US and to gem centers in London, Paris, Amsterdam, and Johannesburg. When New York police detectives were unable to come up with a single clue, the Donahues hired the world-famous Pinkerton Agency to solve the crime.

Neither the police nor the Pinkertons had any luck. The crime remains officially "unsolved" to this day.

UNOFFICIALLY—years later, by his own admission—the identity of the thief did become known. His name was Arthur Barry, arguably the greatest jewel thief in American criminal history. Barry belonged to a class of criminals known in the trade as "second-story men." They were burglars who broke into the second-story bedrooms of the rich to steal their jewelry.

Second-story men considered themselves the kings of thieves. They were often every bit as snobbish as their victims. Barry, for example, only robbed people who were listed in New York's Social Register—a sort of phone book of the rich and famous. Despite its considerable length, he had memorized it all. He referred to his victims as his "clients." His working uniform was a tuxedo and gleaming patent leather shoes. His manners were impeccable, and his knowledge of art and culture impressive.

Barry was known as a man of independent means, and was often invited to lavish parties and gatherings where he was able to meet many of his future "clients." He stole jewels and only jewels—no matter what other opportunities presented themselves as he cased the huge mansions on Long Island that were his favorite hunting ground. According to a 1956 article about him in *Life* Magazine, he was so good-looking and his manner so charming that "wealthy matrons, awakening at night to find him prowling about their bedrooms, often failed to scream."

Barry was resourceful and ingenious. One afternoon, after watching the home of a rich Connecticut industrialist for several weeks and memorizing everyone's routines and schedules, Barry felt ready to pounce. But when he returned to the home that evening, he found that a family member had become seriously ill, the entire house was lit up, and there were relatives and nurses everywhere. He could see it was hopeless.

He knew, however, that the home of Percy Rockefeller was located nearby, and he thought he'd have a quick look at it. The Rockefellers were one of America's wealthiest families, and Percy Rockefeller was very prominent in the Social Register. As expected, the place was enormous, with multiple turrets and chimneys and a high stone wall surrounding the entire estate. More to the point, Barry spotted two bull mastiffs patrolling the lawns—guard dogs probably trained not to accept food from strangers, and to attack at the slightest provocation.

Barry watched them for a while, then continued on home. But the next afternoon he drove back to the Rockefeller house dressed as a telephone lineman. With a small pair of opera glasses, he tracked the mansion's burglar alarm wires to a nearby telephone pole. Climbing the pole, he wired a jumper cable into the line to keep the alarm from sounding at the nearest police station. Then he disconnected the alarm wires that led to the mansion. He could now enter the mansion without triggering the alarm.

That left only those killer dogs to deal with.

To do so, Barry drove to Cos Cob, a nearby township, where he found a dog kennel willing to sell him a female Great Dane for $25. He also purchased a long length of clothesline from a hardware store. That evening, just after dark, he returned to the mansion again.

The lights were out. No one appeared to be home.

Barry waited another hour, keeping careful watch on the windows, the yard, the servants' quarters. Finally he decided it was safe to make a move.

He tied the coil of clothesline onto the Great Dane's collar and hoisted her onto the perimeter wall. Climbing up after her, he lowered her down the other side into the yard and uncoiled the line. The dog promptly disappeared into some nearby bushes. Barry tied the end of the line to a rail on the wall and waited.

He didn't have to wait for long. Moments later, the Rockefeller mastiffs caught the Great Dane's scent and came charging across the lawn. Barry ducked behind a fence pillar and watched. The mastiffs circled the lady excitedly, all thoughts of guard duty gone from their minds.

They looked like they were going to be distracted for quite a while.

Barry chuckled and jumped off the wall into the street. He walked down to the mansion's main gate, jimmied the lock, and walked calmly up the driveway to the front door without getting his shoes dirty. Far down the lawn, he saw that the mastiffs were still frantically wooing the Great Dane.

The next part was simple. Five minutes of searching through the Rockefeller's master bedroom produced $30,000 worth of jewelry. Barry was in and out of the house in less than 10 minutes.

Back on the wall, he reeled in the clothesline and a very flustered Great Dane with it. As he hauled her up to the top of the wall, the mastiffs went berserk with disappointment below.

The next day Barry put on his lineman's uniform, retrieved his jumper cable from the telephone pole, and sold the dog back to the kennel.

When he discovered the theft, Percy Rockefeller hit the roof. He acted nearly as outraged as his mastiffs. He harangued the police department almost daily for months to find the culprit. Finally he hired the William J. Burns Detective Agency to do the job, ordering them to stay on the case until the thief was caught.

They tried their best—but they couldn't come up with a single clue.

And they never did figure out how a burglar could possibly have gotten past two ferocious guard dogs who had been trained not to accept food from strangers.

DURING HIS DECADE-LONG CAREER as a second-story man, Arthur Barry committed more than a thousand burglaries. His thefts were estimated by insurance company agents to exceed $10 million in total—averaging over a million dollars a year. And this was in the 1920s, when a dollar was enough to buy you an entire meal.

The burglary that ended Arthur Barry's career took place on May 29, 1927 in a part of Long Island known as King's Point. Barry had been tipped off by an informant that a large consignment of jewels had just been shipped to the palatial residence of one J. Lauriston Livermore. Livermore was a multimillionaire businessman who had made a fortune in the stock market. He had recently divorced his first wife, and his new "trophy" wife, half his age, was obsessed with diamonds. If she didn't get a fistful of new diamonds every few months, she became very cranky. So Livermore had gotten into the habit of ordering in trays of diamonds from large Manhattan jewelry stores. They were sent to his home "on approval"—the deal being that whichever ones his wife liked, Livermore bought; the rest he sent back.

This latest consignment was easily worth over a million dollars, Barry's informant said. It was being kept in a vault in the furs closet of the Livermores' master bedroom. Livermore's wife usually took a week or so to decide, but they'd been there for several days already, so Barry would have to hurry.

Barry's informant had been reliable in the past, so Barry believed him. Also, Barry had recently taken on an assistant named Monahan, and Monahan was eager to do the job. "A million dollars worth of jewels!" he enthused. "We could take a whole year off and live like kings!"

But when the thieves arrived at the Livermore estate just after dark, they found the Livermores having dinner—with guests.

"We'll just have to wait them out," Barry decided.

At about 9:00 p.m., the two couples (the guests were later identified as Mr. and Mrs. Henry Aronsohn) headed up to their bedrooms. But the lights didn't go out. Fifteen minutes later, everyone appeared at the front door dressed in elegant evening wear. The Livermore limousine drove up, everyone got in, and the limo drove off.

"Damn," Barry swore softly. He'd been studying the two couples with a small pair of binoculars. Livermore's wife had been wearing half a vaultful of jewelry, and Aronsohn's wife had been similarly decked out. This meant that much of what they had come to steal was now in a limousine headed for New York.

"We should wait till they get back," Monahan suggested.

The two men returned to their car and spent the next three hours in a diner in a nearby town called Great Neck.

When they returned, the house was still dark. They had to wait for another half hour before the Livermore limousine returned. "All right," Barry said. "We'll let them get to their bedrooms and turn off their lights."

But the Livermores and their guests weren't ready for bed. For the next two hours they sat in the living room with a fire burning, drinking nightcaps and chatting.

Barry and Monahan sat outside in the shrubbery, shivering.

Finally, at almost three o'clock in the morning, the two couples called it a night.

By now, Barry was regretting he'd ever agreed to this job. Not so much because of the delays and the cold, but because he'd also agreed to do this one "live"—to make it a holdup rather than a simple burglary. Monahan's argument had been that the bulk of the haul was sitting in Livermore's safe, and neither he nor Barry were professional safecrackers. They would need Livermore's cooperation to open it up.

Barry had never conducted a holdup before, but Monahan had a point. So he'd reluctantly agreed.

As soon as the last lights had gone out, the burglars returned to their car for a ladder. Behind them, the house stood black and enormous against the moonlit night, its four tall chimneys looking like small fortresses.

Leaning the ladder gently against the guest bedroom's window frame, Barry climbed up to the window, with Monahan close behind. The window slid up noiselessly. The Aronsohns didn't wake up until Monahan switched on the light.

They sat up abruptly, confused.

"Don't be alarmed," Barry said soothingly. "We won't harm you."

"Who are you?" Aronsohn demanded. His wife shrank against the wall, pulling the comforter up to her chin.

"We just want your jewelry," Barry explained. "We won't be long." He stepped to the dressing table and with quick, practiced moves, found several sets of earrings, some pendants and a diamond bracelet that Mrs. Aronsohn had worn that evening. Not too bad. He pocketed them all.

"I think I'm going to faint," Mrs. Aronsohn exclaimed.

"Oh, don't do that," Barry urged. "Would you like an aspirin?"

"Yes, please."

Barry helped her out of bed, took her to the bathroom, found her some aspirin, and poured her a glass of water. "Now just relax," he said. "All right?"

She nodded.

While Monahan kept an eye on the Aronsohns, Barry continued his search of the room. On top of a bureau he found a man's watch.

"Oh, please don't take that," Aronsohn pleaded. "I got that from my mother. It's not worth much—it's just nickel-plated, not platinum."

"Keep your voice down," Barry said, dropping the watch into his bag. "We've got a couple of lookouts in the yard who'll start shooting if they think there's trouble." He cut the bedside telephone cord with a pair of clippers, and then left the couple under Monahan's guard while he slipped down the hall to the Livermores' bedroom. Their door, however, was locked.

Back in the guest bedroom, he ushered the Aronsohns back into bed and locked the bedroom door. "Now don't make any noise or our men will shoot," he reminded them. "We'll leave your door keys with the Livermores; they'll free you in the morning." Then the two burglars climbed back down their ladder and moved it quietly over to the Livermores' bedroom window.

"Who's there?" Livermore bellowed as Barry came through the window.

"Please be quiet," Barry instructed. He showed Livermore a small pistol. At the sight, Livermore's wife yelped and disappeared under the covers. "We've just come for the jewels," Barry assured them. "The faster we get them, the quicker we'll be out of here."

Livermore looked from Barry to Monahan, then back. He obviously didn't like his options. "Well, take them and get the hell out!" he shouted.

From various shelves and drawers Barry quickly accumulated a growing pile of diamond rings, cufflinks, necklaces, pendants, and bracelets—at least a hundred thousand dollars' worth. He searched until he was fairly sure he'd picked the room clean, then turned to Livermore.

"Now the vault," he said.

"What vault?" Livermore demanded.

"The one in the back of the fur closet," Barry said.

Livermore frowned. "Oh, *that* vault," he said. "There's nothing in it. And anyway, it's jammed."

"I believe you," Barry said. "But I'd like to have a look inside anyway."

"You can't get into it," Livermore insisted. "It's jammed."

Barry pulled out his pistol again. "Don't push me, Mr. Livermore."

Livermore grimaced and got out of bed. He pulled out a drawer in his night table and handed Barry a slip of paper. "There's the combination. Try it yourself if you don't believe me."

Barry spun the dial, clicked in the numbers, then pulled at the door. Nothing happened. He did it again. Still nothing. "We're going to need a hammer," he said to Monahan. Monahan disappeared down the ladder.

A breeze was blowing in through the open window, and Mrs. Livermore shivered. Barry looked around, saw a dressing gown hanging on the bedroom door, and took it down. "Would this help?" he asked courteously.

She pulled it on gratefully. "Thank you very much," she said.

After a few more minutes Barry pointed to several bottles of liquor on a night table. "Would anyone like a drink? This may take awhile."

"Yes, please," Mrs. Livermore said quickly. Livermore shook his head angrily.

Barry poured drinks for himself and Mrs. Livermore. They clinked glasses.

"You're a devil," she said, grinning a little. "Do you know that?"

Her husband glared at her.

Monahan returned, hefting a small sledgehammer he'd found in the Livermore garage. After Barry finished his drink, he turned his attention to the safe. "Please stand back a little," he cautioned Mrs. Livermore, who had moved closer to watch. "There might be flying chips."

He struck the spindle, hard. It flew off in a high arc, clattering to the floor. He got a firm grip on the door handle and pulled sharply. The door swung open.

Empty.

"What did I tell you?" Livermore sneered. "Yeah, there *were* jewels in there last week—a big consignment from New York. But I sent them back a few days ago." He seemed hugely pleased with his triumph.

Barry went back to searching the room.

"Now what are you looking for?" Mrs. Livermore asked.

"Cash," Barry said.

"Why don't I just show you where it is," she said. She went to a closet and opened a small, hidden drawer from under a shelf of women's hats. She pulled out the cash—several hundred dollars' worth—and presented it to Barry.

"You're not really going to take this, are you?" she said. "It's my spending money."

Barry was looking at her collection of hats. "No, you keep it," he said finally. "I like your taste in hats. Buy yourself some veils for them."

Monahan was standing there shaking his head. "Let's go," was all he said.

Mrs. Livermore touched Barry's arm. "You know that diamond and sapphire ring you took," she said. "It was a present from my husband. Could I possibly have that back?"

Barry looked at her for a long moment, then pulled a handful of jewels out of his pocket and gave her back the ring.

"And also my husband's?" she said. Her look was apologetic. "They were a matched set, you see."

Barry grimaced and gave her that ring, too. Then he dug into his other pocket and pulled out Aronsohn's watch. "And you might as well give this watch back to your house guest," he said, handing it to Livermore. "It's made of platinum, not nickel-plate. Tell him he should learn the difference."

He waved and then disappeared down the ladder.

A WEEK LATER, with the newspapers still full of reports about the Livermore robbery, Barry decided it might be safer to get out of town for a while. On their way to the station to take a train up to Lake Ronkonkoma on Long Island, he and his girlfriend Anna met Monahan at a drugstore, where Monahan passed Barry a small leather pouch containing the last few Livermore jewels he hadn't yet been able to sell. They agreed that Barry would hold on to them until he got back from the lake.

For some reason, the train to Ronkonkoma kept encountering delays. The trip, which should have taken about an hour and a half, ended up taking almost four hours. At one point, when the train once again stopped for no obvious reason halfway between Pine-aire and Brentwood, Barry suggested they get off and take a cab to the lake—they were only a few miles away. But Anna took too long to decide, and the train began moving again.

It was a fateful error.

At Ronkonkoma Station, Barry was met by three men who immediately surrounded him and flashed their badges. They searched him and found the pouch with the stolen jewels. It turned out that Monahan and his wife had been having marital problems, and his wife had betrayed her husband and his partner to the police. The train's delays had been ordered by the Nassau County police captain, to enable his detectives to get to the Ronkonkoma Station to arrest Barry.

Even this evidence probably wouldn't have been enough to sink Arthur Barry; he was normally very careful and had a clean police record. But his agreement to rob the Livermores "live" proved his undoing, because the couple had no trouble identifying him as their thief in a police line-up.

Barry was sentenced to 25 years in prison. He served 19 years of his sentence, and was finally paroled in 1949 at the age of 53.

THREE YEARS LATER, in 1952, Barry—now the manager of a chain of dairy bars in Massachusetts—was asked by a parent-teacher association on Long Island to give them an inspirational talk on "juvenile delinquency." In an effort to go straight and to gain a reputation as an honest man, Barry had taken to accepting such invitations.

That evening, after his talk, a well-dressed, middle-aged woman came up to him. "Do you remember me?" she asked.

Barry looked at her carefully. "No," he finally admitted. "Should I?"

She smiled. "Let me help you remember," she said. "Do you recall an evening when you returned my spending money and complimented me on my taste in hats?"

"Dorothy Livermore!" Barry exclaimed. "You're Mrs. Livermore."

"Yes, I am," she agreed. "And I came quite a distance to hear you." She took his hand in both of hers and pressed it warmly.

They looked at each other frankly, honestly. Barry felt

suddenly very moved. Dorothy Livermore had been his final victim—the last "client" of Arthur Barry, Master Jewel Thief. He supposed he should be angry with her; her identification of him in a police line-up had cost him 19 long years in prison. But it was only a fleeting thought. He had always made his own choices, and he had finally suffered the consequences. It was over now. He knew, suddenly, with a certainty he hadn't had until now, that he would never be a jewel thief again.

Dorothy Livermore unclasped her hands. "I'm glad you're doing well, Mr. Barry," she said simply. "I'm *relieved* you're doing well."

He didn't move until she had disappeared through the door and out into the night.

JUST AFTER MIDNIGHT on August 8, 1963, a convoy of 15 men in two Land Rovers and an army truck drove stealthily along the back roads of rural Buckinghamshire in southern England. A low-lying mist swirled around the vehicles, but the sky above them was clear and studded with stars. They were headed for the Bridego Bridge, a small railway overpass located about 40 miles (65 km) northwest of London on British Rail's Glasgow-to-London line.

The men in the trucks all wore army uniforms, because there was a military base nearby and local residents were accustomed to seeing military vehicles patrolling the roads. In the lead Land Rover, dressed in a major's uniform, was Bruce Reynolds, a tall bespectacled man who wore leather gloves and had a military mustache. He had the swashbuckling air of a paratroop commander and always drove fast British sports cars. He was the leader of a gang of thieves known around London as the Southwest Gang (aka The Brighton Boys). Four of them sat squeezed onto the bench seat behind him. Two others drove the army truck that was staying right on the Land Rover's tail.

The gang in the second Land Rover—known around London as the Southeast Gang (aka The Heavies)—was led by a short fat man named Buster Edwards. Unlike Reynolds, who preferred fancy hotels, classy restaurants, and holidays in the south of France, Edwards was a cheerful, hard-drinking meat-and-potatoes man who spent his nights carousing and fighting in rowdy bars and nightclubs. He was by nature generous and warm-hearted, but he could be ruthless when the situation called for it. His five men were all squashed into the Rover's rear seat and luggage compartment behind him.

Teaming up was something that London's criminal gangs almost never did. Each gang controlled its own part of London, and kept a sharp lookout for signs that a rival gang might be poaching on its territory. But this was a very special job. It required a lot of smarts, technical expertise, inside information, and muscle—far too much for one gang alone. Besides, Reynolds and Edwards had been confederates on a number of other jobs in earlier times and they trusted each other. So the two gangs had made an exception and joined forces.

WHEN THE VEHICLES ARRIVED at the bridge—around 2:00 a.m.—they were quickly hidden in the nearby bush. Then the men hauled out railway coveralls and pulled them on over their army uniforms. Within minutes, they had all been transformed into a team of railway workers on night shift.

Up on the rail bed, four sets of railway tracks glistened eerily in the moonlight. The only sound was the occasional bark of a dog from one of the farms nearby. In the distance, about half a mile (a kilometer) up the tracks, four green lights glowed dimly on a gantry hanging over the rails. These lights indicated that the lines were clear for all London-bound traffic.

There was a small utility shack near the bridge, which Edwards' men broke into. They hauled out axes, sledgehammers, and crowbars. Reynolds distributed two-way radios to a number of men from both gangs, then took two men with him up the track to the gantry. This was a narrow metal gangway built across the width of the rail bed at a height of about 25 feet (8 m). It had a traffic signal (red, amber, green) hanging over each set of rails. Metal foot pegs enabled a maintenance man to climb up and walk across above the tracks, to service the four signals.

One of the men stayed at the gantry while Reynolds and the other man headed for a dwarf signal another half mile farther along. This was a warning signal, intended to alert the engineer of a fast-moving train that a signal change was coming up at the next gantry. A lit-up amber light in a dwarf signal told engineers to slow their trains to a crawl.

Reynolds turned on his radio. "Can you hear me?" he asked in a low voice.

There was a small burst of static and then Edwards's faint response: "I hear you."

"We're at the dwarf, and I'm heading up to the next bend."

"Roger," came the brief reply.

Reynolds left his last man at the dwarf signal and continued up the track. Beyond the next bend, he'd be able to see any approaching London-bound train from several miles away.

Not long after he'd rounded the bend, he radioed a warning. "It's now 2:53, chaps. Only 10 more minutes. She'll be coming through on track two."

Back at the gantry, everyone pulled on gloves and ski masks and took up positions. Edwards and his Heavies lay down flat on the embankment just below the gantry, keeping their heads low. Several Brighton Boys measured out the place where the back end of the second railcar would come to a stop, and lay down on the embankment below that spot. Several more ran to the army truck and got ready to back it out of the bush and up against the embankment.

Reynold's man at the gantry climbed up the foot pegs and

opened the signal box over Track #2. He covered the lit-up green light with an old glove, blacking it out. Then he connected a small battery pack to the unlit bulb in the red light and turned it on. The signal on the gantry for Track #2 now shone bright red.

While he was doing this, the man at the dwarf signal shimmied up the pole and blacked out its green light in the same way. Then he attached a battery pack to the amber light and switched it on. The signal on the dwarf signal for Track #2 now shone bright amber.

At 3:02 a.m. everyone's radio crackled. "Here she comes, chaps," Reynold's voice announced. "Get ready. This is it."

Soon the thrum of an approaching train began to vibrate through the tracks. Then they could hear it—a faint rumble approaching rapidly through the night, growing louder by the second. The ground began to tremble. A minute later a huge D-type diesel locomotive came thundering around the bend, its powerful headlight lighting up the surrounding forest with a long, cone-shaped glare. The light widened quickly until it flooded the entire area with such brilliant intensity that Reynolds, still at the bend, found himself automatically crouching closer to the ground. The rumble turned into a roar and then the light fell abruptly, replaced by a loud screeching of steel on steel and a spray of sparks as the locomotive pounded past, its wheels straining against the curve. Behind the locomotive, a long string of glowing pinpricks indicated the tiny windows of the 14 railcars that made up the Royal Mail Train.

A rising squeal of brakes indicated that the engineer had seen the amber dwarf signal ahead, and had begun to slow down.

By the time the last railcar had passed the dwarf signal, it was rolling along at little more than walking speed. At the gantry, the locomotive gave off an explosion of shrieks and hisses as it came to a grinding stop.

The Royal Mail Train now towered motionless above the gang, its engines throbbing powerfully. Its cab windows glowed like a giant cat's eyes. Trailing away into the dark was its long tail of cars, behind whose closed doors and tiny windows over 70 men and women in postal uniforms were busily sorting the mail, paying no attention to the train's stops and starts.

A small door in the side of the cab opened and a fireman climbed down the metal ladder. He jumped the last 6 feet (2 m) to the ground and, since British trains in the 1960s weren't yet outfitted with radios, headed toward a telephone box at the side of the tracks.

Edwards stood up and the fireman caught sight of him. "What's up, mate?" he asked.

"Problem up ahead," Edwards said, waving a piece of paper. "Have a look at this." The fireman crossed the tracks to look. As he reached Edwards, the rest of The Heavies stood up and grabbed him. "Any noise and you're dead," Edwards warned the fireman, while two others quickly tied him up and dragged him down the embankment. The fireman made no effort to resist.

Back at the locomotive, one of the gang members made a stirrup of his hands and hoisted Edwards up to the bottom of the cab's ladder. At that moment, the engineer appeared in the doorway above them. "Get away from that ladder!" he snarled.

Realizing the engineer must have seen the attack on his fireman from the window, Edwards didn't answer. He heaved himself up the ladder two rungs at a time. As he reached the bottom of the cab's doorway, the engineer kicked frantically at his hands on the rungs. Edwards swore, but kept coming. Soon the two men were grappling awkwardly at the top of the ladder, and Edwards might have lost his footing if one of his men hadn't run around the front of the train and climbed into the cab from the other side. Suddenly the engineer was grabbed from behind and fell back yelling; Edwards was instantly on top of him. He hit the engineer's head with a small pellet-filled pouch called a blackjack. The blow split the man's scalp, releasing a gush of blood. He promptly gave up.

Meanwhile, two Brighton Boys had slipped underneath the train and were busily disconnecting the couplings and vacuum hoses at the end of the second car. Their "inside man," a postal employee who had never given them his name—they simply called him "the Ulsterman" because of his northern Irish accent—had told them that on Royal Mail trains of this type, only the second car contained what the gangs were after: mail sacks full of money being shipped back to London from banks all along the line.

Edwards stuck his head out of the cab doorway and looked down. "You boys ready down there?"

"All clear!" came the reply.

"All right," Edwards said to the engineer, who was sitting on the floor, wiping the blood off his face with his handkerchief. "Here's what you're going to do. You're going to move this train forward to the bridge up ahead, and you're going to stop it exactly when I tell you to, or you'll get another whack of my blackjack. You got that?"

"All right," the engineer said. "I got it."

He stumbled over to the driver's seat and sat down at the controls. He turned several handles to release the brakes and pulled on the throttle. The engines behind them burst into a roar.

But nothing moved.

"Move the damn train," Edwards said in a threatening tone.

"I'm trying," the engineer protested. "I don't know what's wrong. Did somebody release the vacuum?"

Suddenly there was a loud screech of metal as the accordion connection between the second and third cars ripped apart. The locomotive began to move.

"What the hell was that?" the engineer demanded.

"None of your business," Edwards assured him. "Just keep it moving."

Disconnected from the 12 other cars, the locomotive and its first two cars quickly picked up speed. Within minutes they had reached the bridge.

"All right," Edwards said. "Now slow down, and stop right when we get to the end of the bridge. When we get to that little shed at the end of the bridge. Stop it right....now!"

The engineer reversed throttle and cranked on the brakes. The train ground to a halt once more.

"All right," Edwards said. "Your job is over now. Relax."

He left the engineer in the hands of one of his Heavies and climbed off the train.

OUTSIDE IT WAS BECOMING NOTICEABLY LIGHTER as morning approached. The stars were fading and the ground fog across the surrounding fields had lifted. You could see the outlines of barns and farmhouses almost to the horizon by now.

Reynolds was already over at the utility shed, handing out the sledgehammers and crowbars. "Good job, chaps," he said. "Well done. Now for the payoff."

From the Ulsterman, they knew that the first car would

contain nothing but regular mail, with no one inside. The second car, however, would have half a dozen sorters working in it. They would have to be taken by storm.

Reynolds gave the signal. The men quickly attacked the car from every side. Windows splintered, doors were smashed in, ventilation shafts were ripped out. Within minutes the car was breached. The first men in found the sorters frantically piling mail sacks against the doors and windows in a desperate attempt to repel their invaders. They were all quickly subdued and tied up at the back of the railcar. Then the men turned to a large metal cage by the car's front door.

That, the Ulsterman had assured them, was where the money would be.

A single blow from a sledgehammer broke off the lock.

Inside, they found a large pile of white canvas mail sacks. Each was full to bursting and identified with a pink tag labeled HVP.

"High Value Package," Reynolds murmured. "God bless the Ulsterman."

One of the men dragged out a sack and sliced it open. An armful of tightly packed bundles fell out.

Banknotes!

Great fat bundles of used, untraceable banknotes!

The men gave a cheer.

"All right," Reynolds grinned. "Let's get on with it. We're running low on time here, chaps."

Everyone quickly formed a human chain from the railcar to the army truck that had been backed against the embankment below.

The sacks were a lot heavier than they looked. Soon everyone was dripping with sweat. It wasn't long before some of the men were stumbling and falling. Sacks were dropped. Men stopped to catch their breath. Someone got the bright idea of simply rolling the sacks down the embankment and that helped, but by the time Reynolds called a halt, several of the men looked ready for a heart attack. A few of the sacks had rolled off into the bush, but nobody had the energy to chase after them. What were 20,000 or 30,000 pounds when there were millions more in the truck? They had loaded up 120 sacks full of banknotes. It had to be the haul of the century.

BY THE TIME they were ready to leave, it was dangerously late. The sun was almost up and the roosters on nearby farms were crowing. Abandoning the train, the men hastily pulled off their railway coveralls and became military personnel again. Someone hauled out a police radio and tuned it to the frequency of the Buckinghamshire police, but there were no announcements about the robbery yet. The three vehicles retraced their previous route in convoy, heading back to Leatherslade Farm. This hideout, which was about 30 miles (50 km) away in Oxfordshire, had been bought for them by a crooked lawyer several months earlier.

At the farm, the men hid the army truck in the barn and dragged tarps over the Land Rovers. In the farmhouse, they positioned a guard with binoculars at each attic window to keep a lookout on the surrounding countryside. Everyone kept their gloves on to avoid leaving fingerprints. Jubilant but exhausted, most of the men dropped down on mattresses strewn around the house and quickly fell asleep.

By the following morning, news of the daring robbery had spread throughout the entire country. Every radio station seemed obsessed with it. Radio announcers expressed amazement at the gang's sophistication and military precision. A crime historian admitted he couldn't recall a robbery in the history of British crime that had involved so many criminals and so much money. Callers expressed astonishment and outrage that criminals had had the gall to attack one of the country's most sacred public trusts. "I mean, I can understand banks, or businesses, or maybe even the odd lorry [truck]," one caller protested. "But robbing the Royal Mail! That's right over the top, mate!"

The British Broadcasting Corporation called it the crime of the century.

After half an hour of sampling the public stations, the men turned to their police radio and listened to its barrage of bulletins and messages, trying to figure out what the police might be thinking. So far, however, they seemed to be completely baffled.

Reynolds had predicted that the police would assume the thieves to be Londoners, who would flee back to their home base immediately after the robbery. That's why he had arranged for the purchase of Leatherslade Farm. The plan was to stay holed up at the farm until the police discovered they were wrong and shifted their attention from London to other cities—something Reynolds expected would happen in three to four days. Then the robbers could slip back to London under cover of darkness.

By lunchtime, everyone was in high spirits. Someone tuned in a radio station that featured Tony Bennett singing "It's the Good Life" and everyone chimed in. Reynolds, Edwards, and several of the other thieves who had a good head for numbers brewed themselves cups of tea and began to count the bundles of banknotes.

Someone else had brought a Monopoly set, and soon half a dozen thieves were playing the game boisterously, using real money. It wasn't long before an entire case of whisky had been consumed.

By suppertime, the count was complete—and it was impressive! A pile of over 2.5 million pounds' worth of banknotes rose all the way to the living room ceiling. It was enough to give every gang member a share of 150,000 pounds—an amount that would be worth over 5 million dollars today.

That was the good news.

The bad news was that as the day progressed, it became increasingly clear from the radio bulletins that the police hadn't assumed the thieves had fled to London. In fact, they appeared to have assumed the very opposite. A house-to-house search was now underway in an ever widening circle around Bridego Bridge.

It would only be a matter of time before the searchers arrived at Leatherslade Farm.

At this point, some of the thieves became panicky, and the group's discipline began to fray. According to the original plan, the three to four days after the robbery were supposed to be spent getting rid of evidence such as the mail sacks, the uniforms, and the vehicles. The farmhouse was to be swept clean of any fingerprints or other identifiers. But, by the end of the second day, most of the thieves had taken off, and the cleanup was left to the lawyer who had purchased the farm for the gang.

This lawyer, for reasons that remain hard to understand, decided to hire a man named Mark to do this very important job.

It would prove to be a mistake he would deeply regret.

Either Mark didn't appreciate the urgency, or he wasn't told. Whatever the reason, when Reynolds and Edwards called on the lawyer at his London office the next day to verify that the job had been done, the lawyer admitted he had only just heard from Mark—and Mark hadn't yet been out to the farm!

The two men looked stunned. Then Edwards hurled himself across the lawyer's desk, reaching for his throat. He might have throttled the poor man if Reynolds hadn't pulled him off, reminding him that they had more important things to worry about. Both ran out to the parking lot, leaped into Reynolds's sports car and roared off toward Oxfordshire in a desperate effort to stave off disaster.

But it was too late.

Halfway to Cheddington, a news bulletin on the radio announced that police investigators had discovered what they assumed to be the train robbers' hideout. At a place called Leatherslade Farm, they had found three military vehicles, a pile of partially burned and buried uniforms, and a large number of white canvas mail sacks filled with banknote wrappings.

Reynolds and Edwards looked at each other wordlessly.

"I think we're bloody nicked," Edwards said finally.

EDWARDS WAS RIGHT. Although many of the gang members quickly fled England for places as far away as Australia, Mexico, Brazil, and Canada, and even though several even underwent plastic surgery to alter their appearance, they were picked up by Scotland Yard one after another.

As more and more damning evidence was found, extradition orders were issued. The fingerprint experts who dusted the locomotive, the gantry, the vehicles, and the entire farm found prints for almost everyone. Edwards was identified by a single print left on a banknote wrapper. Reynolds had left a fingerprint on the Monopoly board. Articles of clothing, keys—even a mere spot of paint on a shoe—brought down man after man.

By the middle of September—only five weeks later—five of the thieves had been arrested and warrants had been issued for five more. By year's end, nine were in custody, and by the following spring, when the first trials began, 11 men had been "nicked."

And now the robbers made their second big mistake—they let themselves be blinded by their skyrocketing fame. Newspapers and television stations all over the western world had dubbed their heist "The Great Train Robbery" and made many of the gang members into media heroes. As a result, public demand for seats at the trial was so great, there were reports of people secretly "selling" their places in the courtroom for as much as 50 pounds a day. Journalists from all over Britain and from as far away as Australia and Japan clamored for courtroom passes.

If the trial had been held in London's most famous court-house, the Old Bailey, this fame might have helped influence the judge or jury to take a more lenient view of the gang's crimes. But judicial authorities decided to hold the trial in the town of Aylesbury, in Buckinghamshire where the crime had been committed. The gang members—or at least their lawyers—should have realized that the citizens of this modest little town weren't as likely to be impressed by media heroes or their high-priced lawyers.

Instead, they ignored the judge, mocked the jury, and hammed it up for the media's cameras and tape recorders. During interviews with the press, they announced confidently that they expected sentences of no worse than five to seven years—ten years at the very most. Since little of the stolen money had been recovered, the press drew the obvious conclusion: gang members expected to spend a few years in jail, then be set free to enjoy their ill-gotten gains in luxury for years to come.

It didn't turn out that way.

Judge Edmund Davis of the Aylesbury Assize Court was not amused by these big-city attitudes. Gang members got their first taste of just how unamused he was when he passed sentence on Roger John Codrey, the only gang member who had pleaded guilty and therefore expected to receive the most lenient sentence. "You are the first to be sentenced out of 11 greedy men whom hope of gain allured," the judge pronounced. "You have all been convicted of a crime which in its impudence and enormity is the first of its kind in this country. I propose to do all within my power to make sure it will also be the last."

He sentenced Codrey to 20 years.

There were gasps throughout the courtroom. The lawyers were stunned, the press amazed. Even the gang members found it hard to look as if they didn't care.

And there was worse to follow. As gang member after gang member stood up to receive his sentence, the judgments came down like hammer blows: 24 years, 25 years, 30 years, 30 years, 30 years, 30 years.

In the end, eight of the accused gang members received sentences of 30 years. Most of the rest received 20 to 25 years.

And if the gang had hopes that these harsh sentences might be overturned on appeal, they were in for another disappointment. At their appeal hearing six months later, the judge announced that he considered the robbing of a Royal Mail Train as reaching "new depths of lawlessness for which the type of sentence normally imposed for armed robbery is inadequate." He denied all but two appeals, and confirmed every single 30-year sentence.

During the next three years, the last four train robbers were caught, and all received 30-year sentences. By 1969, all but one were firmly behind bars. This last holdout—Ronald Biggs—had been part of the first group of robbers to be tried and sentenced, and he had received 30 years. But he escaped from Wandsworth Prison in 1965, and led Scotland Yard on a merry international chase that lasted an astonishing 36 years. But even Biggs finally became too homesick for England to stay on the run forever. He turned himself in voluntarily in 2001, and was sentenced to serve the rest of his original prison term—28 years.

Although Scotland Yard did finally catch all the robbers, it didn't do nearly so well with the money. In the end, only 200,000 pounds—a tiny fraction of the train robbers' haul—was ever recovered. For years, people wondered: what happened to all that money?

Now that all the robbers except Biggs have been released, investigative journalists have been able to get to the bottom of that last question, too. What they found was perhaps not altogether unexpected: the gangs' lawyers got most of it. The trials lasted so long, and the appeals were so expensive, that much of the money was spent on legal defense.

But much of what remained—money the robbers had buried or entrusted to friends until their release—met with an even more ironic fate. It was stolen by other thieves while the train robbers were in jail!

So much for the old saying that there is "honor among thieves."

The Many Faces of Willie Sutton

WILLIE SUTTON NEVER TOOK SHORTCUTS.

Take the Converse Bank in Long Island, New York. For weeks during the fall of 1921, Sutton had been casing this bank, carefully keeping a detailed record of when its employees arrived and what routines each person followed. He even knew their names, plus the names of their spouses and their children.

The bank was opened each morning by a guard at 8:00 a.m. This guard admitted the bank's six clerks and tellers, who arrived around 8:15 a.m. The guard always identified the employees through the windows in the upper part of the front doors, then let them in. The manager arrived about 15 minutes later.

Few bank robbers in the 1920s prepared their robberies as carefully as Willie Sutton. Most just barged in waving tommy guns and revolvers. But Sutton was both a professional and a perfectionist. He considered casing a bank as important as actually robbing it. While casing it, he never watched a bank from the same place twice. Some days he watched it from his car; others from a park bench or a bus stop. And he changed his clothes and appearance every day. You never knew what might attract someone's attention.

It was this obsession with detail that made Sutton's robberies look effortless. After weeks of painstaking preparation, the robbery itself rarely took more than 15 or 20 minutes.

On the day Sutton decided he was finally ready to rob the

Converse Bank, he got up at 5:30 a.m. He sat down in front of his bathroom mirror and opened his makeup kit. Sutton had always been fascinated by the theater, and years of dating show-girls had taught him how to change his appearance in a hundred different ways. He worked carefully, applying eyeliner, rouge, and charcoal in subtle ways. Sometimes he added a mole or a scar. Sometimes he pushed small pieces of hollowed-out cork up his nostrils. He had boxes full of hairpieces, mustaches, eye-brows, and sideburns. He could make himself look years older or years younger, fat or thin, bald or hairy. The whole idea was to be unrecognizable if witnesses tried to identify him later in a police line-up.

Today he made himself look as young as possible because he was going in as a Western Union bank messenger.

Sutton's nickname in the bank robbing trade was "The Actor." He had become famous all over North America for his ingenious robberies using disguises. He had whole closets full of uniforms and costumes in his New York apartment that he used exclusively for bank robbing. His most common disguise was that of a policeman, but he'd also had success as a fireman, an army officer, a pilot, a chauffeur, and even a window-washer.

When his face was made up, Sutton selected a neat-looking khaki outfit, inconspicuous and conservative, with a box cap— exactly what a self-respecting bank messenger would wear. He chose a big briefcase of the sort bank messengers usually carried. Then he steamed open a Western Union envelope containing a telegram he'd sent to himself the day before. He threw the telegram away, and substituted a similarly colored yellow sheet on which he'd typed the name of the Converse Bank's manager and the bank's address. He'd typed them so they appeared in exactly the right place in the envelope window.

Sometimes Sutton worked alone and sometimes he used helpers. For today's job, he had teamed up with Jack Bassett, a man who had joined him in a number of previous robberies. By 7:50 a.m., the two men were ready and waiting in a parking lot within sight of the bank.

Shortly after the guard entered the bank at 8:00 a.m., Sutton appeared at the bank's front door in his disguise, briefcase in hand. He rang the bell.

The guard opened the door a tiny slit. "The bank's not open yet."

"Western Union," Sutton said. He spoke with a slight lisp, to confuse potential witnesses later. "Got a telegram for the boss."

Seeing the uniform and the envelope, the guard opened the door wider. Sutton handed him the telegram, a pen, and a small notebook. "Could you sign for it?"

The guard took the notebook with his left hand and began to sign with his right. The instant his hands were both occupied, Sutton reached down and lifted the guard's revolver out of his holster.

"Okay, my good man," he said, poking the muzzle into the guard's stomach. "Just do what I tell you and you won't get hurt."

The guard looked startled. He took several bewildered steps back. Sutton quickly followed him in. At the same moment, Jack Bassett, who'd been waiting nearby, slipped through the door behind Sutton and closed it.

It was now 8:06 a.m.

Sutton took off his messenger's hat but kept the revolver cocked. "I know you've got six employees who are going to show up any minute, Fred," he said to the guard. "Let everyone in exactly as usual. No funny business, or believe me, I'll use this." The guard looked at the gun and shrugged hopelessly. Sutton could see he was perplexed at how this bank robber knew his name. Bassett carried in half a dozen chairs and lined them up against the wall.

At 8:13 a.m., the bell rang for the first time. The guard looked through the window, then opened the door. The first clerk walked in. "Lovely day, Fred," he said cheerfully.

"That's what you think," the guard mumbled.

The clerk looked surprised—and then he saw the bank robbers. Before he could react, Bassett took him by the arm, led him to a chair, and sat him down. "Just sit tight and don't try anything," he warned.

The next arrival was a young teller in a summer dress. "'Lo, Fred," she said happily, swinging her purse in circles around her arm. She stopped swinging abruptly.

Ten minutes later, the chairs were full. At 8:30 a.m., Harry, the manager, arrived.

This was always the trickiest part of a bank heist. Ordinary bank employees rarely caused trouble, but managers could be unpredictable. At the sight of the robbers, Harry spun around and rushed for the door. He was fast, but not quite fast enough. Bassett cut him off, and Sutton took a firm hold of his shoulder. He made sure to speak to him loudly enough for his employees to hear.

"Listen to me, Harry. All I want you to do is open the vault," he said. "It would be very foolish of you to refuse. If you do refuse, you won't be hurt, but some of your employees will be shot. Do you understand? Their welfare is in your hands. It's up to you."

This put the manager into exactly the fix Sutton intended. A threat aimed at himself might not have much effect—he looked as if he might be prepared to risk his life for the sake of his reputation with the bank. But the lives of his employees were another matter. Now they were looking at him expectantly—anxiously. One teller was crying; another appeared hysterical.

The look in the manager's eyes gave him away. He realized he was boxed in. "I guess I don't have much choice," he said grudgingly.

"You're dead right about that," Sutton agreed.

The clock on the wall showed 8:46 a.m.

While Bassett kept everyone else under guard, the manager led Sutton to the vault. All that was visible of it was a huge dial set into a flat metal door. The manager hesitated. "Let's keep this moving," Sutton warned, prodding him gently with Fred's gun. The bank was slated to open in 12 minutes. Sutton knew there would already be customers gathering at the door.

When the vault door swung open, Sutton quickly surveyed the metal boxes stacked on its shelves. His instinct about where the cash was kept was rarely wrong. He zeroed in on some small footlockers on the lowest shelf. Bingo. He scooped their large-denomination banknotes into his briefcase. Now the reserves. He pointed at a small safe on a shelf higher up. The manager looked disappointed, but opened it without a word. Sutton quickly emptied its contents. The total take looked to be about $250,000.

"Now here's the drill," Sutton explained when everyone was reunited in the lobby. "We've got a third member of our gang outside, with a rifle trained on the bank's front door. If anyone runs out that door during the next five minutes, he'll be shot. Everybody got that? Everyone stay inside for a full five minutes, and you'll be just fine."

Sutton knew perfectly well that the instant he and Bassett

went out the door, the manager would be on the phone to the police. But it would take the police at least 10 minutes to get here. That was all the time Sutton and Barrett needed to escape. He just didn't want anyone running after them, raising an instant alarm.

The bank employees obeyed his order. (They usually did.) At exactly 8:55 a.m., Bassett and Sutton slipped out the bank's front door and were quickly absorbed by the crowds on Jamaica Avenue.

Right on time. No violence. No hysteria. And a fat payoff.

It was a trademark Sutton robbery.

WILLIE SUTTON had been raised in Irishtown, a rough, tough part of Brooklyn. His father was a blacksmith and his mother was very religious. No one in the Sutton family had ever been in trouble with the police before Willie began to go wrong.

As a kid, Willie had actually wanted to become a criminal lawyer. He'd made that decision after his father was hit by a delivery truck in lower Manhattan, which broke his collarbone. The driver was drunk, so his father hired an attorney and sued. Everyone said he had an excellent case, and the Sutton family expected to be well compensated for his pain, suffering, and medical bills. But before the case could go to trial, the attorney inexplicably settled with the insurance company for a few hundred dollars. He convinced the family that they were lucky to get even that much. The family believed him, but some time later they discovered that the attorney had been on the insurance company's payroll. It was apparently a common arrangement in the 1920s. That's when Willie decided to become a criminal lawyer—to defend people like his father against insurance companies.

But the Sutton family was poor, and a legal education expensive. What happened instead was that at age 15, Willie found himself working for pennies as a lowly messenger boy in a bank. His experience there simply increased his anger against the big financial institutions that seemed to thrive on taking advantage of poor people. "I'd see these poor people coming in early in the morning, putting their nickels and dimes in their accounts," he later wrote in his memoir *Where the Money Was: Memoirs of a Bank Robber.* "And then at about eleven o'clock the bank president would be driven up in his limousine, his chauffeur would open the door for him and in he would come—morning clothes, derby hat, cane hooked over his arm—nodding at everybody without looking at anybody—it just infuriated me."

Willie began taking revenge by stealing rolls of postage stamps from his employer, but he soon progressed to much bigger thefts. He received his early instruction in robbing jewelry stores and then banks from a local safecracker and lockpicker named Doc Tate. The Doc approached his specialty like a surgeon, always wearing ultra-thin leather gloves to protect his sensitive fingertips. From Doc Tate, Sutton learned how to break into a safe by all the conventional methods of the day: picking a lock by feel, cracking it with a punch or jimmy, drilling it open—or, when all else failed, blowing it up with dynamite.

The problem was, the companies that manufactured safes kept improving their product. Their locks became increasingly more difficult to pick. The metals used to manufacture safes became harder to cut with a torch, and even harder to drill. There came a point in Sutton's bank robbing career when these difficulties became so challenging, he decided there had to be an easier way.

There was—and Sutton discovered it one afternoon as he

was walking along Broadway in New York City. Half a block ahead of him, an armored truck stopped in front of a bank. Two uniformed guards marched up to a secured entrance, rang the bell, and were promptly let in. A few minutes later, they emerged from the bank hauling heavy bags of cash. They flung them into their truck and drove away.

That little incident changed Sutton's life—and his method of bank robbing. After a dozen years of breaking, sawing, smashing, and blasting his way into banks, he suddenly realized there was a far easier way to get the job done.

You just put on the right uniform!

It made such simple sense. Bank employees were virtually programmed to view people in uniform as part of the team when they knocked on a bank door. A uniform announced the knocker's identity more loudly than any piece of paper or badge. In fact, Sutton suspected that the clerk who had let those uniformed guards into the bank hadn't even bothered to look at their faces. Their uniforms alone had convinced him.

It was, Sutton discovered, one of the most basic tactics of the martial arts. You learned how to use your opponent's unconscious reactions to defeat him.

Sutton discovered there were other advantages to this approach as well. Once you were inside the bank, a little psychology could take you a lot farther than a blowtorch or dynamite. There were at least three people on every bank employee roster who knew the combination to the bank's vault. Why smash and drill and blast away at a vault for half a night when there were three people sitting in front of you who could do the job for you in just a few seconds? You simply had to come up with an argument that convinced them to do it on your behalf.

Ingenuity and psychology instead of brute force. Surprise

and audacity instead of violence. This more modern approach to bankrobbing formed the basis for Sutton's eventual fame.

Sutton immediately set to work to develop the details of this new approach. He rented a room in the Broadway theater district under the name Waverly School of Drama. He ordered letterhead and business cards. Then he typed out a letter on his new stationery, saying that the school was putting on an amateur play and wanted to rent a policeman's uniform. He sent this letter to half a dozen costume rental companies.

Every rental company replied. They all assured Sutton they could provide complete satisfaction. All the Waverly School of Drama had to do was send their actors in for a fitting. Costumes could be adjusted to any size.

Sutton selected a costume house and rang for an appointment. What he saw when he was ushered in made his mouth water. Costumes of every conceivable description—rows and rows of them! For policemen's uniforms alone, the house offered 23 different kinds.

Over the following 34 years, Sutton used such costumes to rob well over a hundred banks. In fact, he used costumes so often he really began to feel like an actor. When he put on the uniform of a mailman, he *became* a dedicated member of the US Postal Service. Neither hail nor sleet nor rain nor snow was going to keep him from delivering his special-delivery letter to that bank. When he put on a policeman's uniform, he found himself unconsciously checking the doors of the shops he was passing on his way to the bank. He found himself waving in a comradely way to other policemen who were directing traffic or patrolling the street. When a motorist asked him whether he could briefly leave his car in a no-parking zone, Sutton gave the man a stern lecture about obeying city bylaws!

Once, when Sutton was disguised as a policeman and was crossing a street on his way to rob a bank in Philadelphia, a passing police captain stopped him and bawled him out for having a loose button on his collar. "The amazing thing was," Sutton recalled later, "I felt just awful about that button. Yes, sir, you're right, sir, it's an absolute disgrace, sir. I found that the minute I put on that uniform, I was an utterly conscientious cop—right up until I got to the bank. Once I got to the bank, I stopped being a conscientious cop and became a conscientious thief!"

PERHAPS SUTTON'S MOST INGENIOUS bank heist involving a disguise came in 1934, when he took aim at the Ozone Park Bank in Brooklyn. Casing the bank in his usual methodical way, he discovered two important facts. First, the manager looked surprisingly like Sutton himself. Second, the manager preferred double-breasted, gray pinstriped suits.

When Sutton finally decided how he would "take" this bank, he built his strategy around those two facts.

Instead of his normal method of hitting a bank *before* most of its staff had arrived, Sutton waited until the bank opened at 8:30 a.m., then walked in like an ordinary customer. He stayed just long enough to determine exactly what the manager was wearing, and how he was looking that day. Then he returned home.

He spent the next three hours painstakingly making himself look like that manager—same hair color, same shirt color, similar tie, mustache, suit. Then he waited in a café across the street until he saw the manager leave for lunch.

Two minutes later, Sutton swept into the bank. He headed straight for "his" office, acting as if he'd just briefly come back for something he'd forgotten. He picked up "his" briefcase, walked into the vault with it, loaded it up with over $100,000 in large-denomination banknotes—and calmly walked out again.

The whole undertaking had taken less than five minutes. No one had challenged him, no one had spoken to him, no one had paid any attention to him. In fact, the theft wasn't even discovered until almost an hour after the real manager had returned!

BY THE TIME he was 45 years old, Willie Sutton had been number one on the FBI's Most Wanted list for many years. During that time, he had been caught half a dozen times and sentenced to an aggregate total of almost 100 years in prison. But he kept escaping, finding new partners, and robbing more banks. He kept robbing banks even after he'd stolen and squirreled away so much money, he could have retired in luxury on some South Pacific island.

A psychologist at Sing Sing Prison had warned Sutton about this. "Banks will always present you with an irresistible challenge, Willie," he had said. "You won't be able to walk past a bank without automatically starting to case it." And it was true. Sutton admitted it himself.

"When all is said and done, I robbed banks because I really enjoyed it," he wrote in his memoir. "I was more alive when I was inside a bank, robbing it, than at any other time in my life. I enjoyed everything about it so much that no matter how much I scored, one or two weeks later I'd be out there looking for my next job. Even when it might cost me more than I could possibly hope to gain."

That eventually happened later in 1934, when Sutton was caught and sent to Eastern State Penitentiary on a sentence of 50 years. For 11 years he tried desperately to break out of this prison—everything from swimming through its rat-infested sewers to crawling through its blistering heating ducts. He even teamed up with a dozen other inmates to dig a 3,000-foot (1000-m) tunnel under the prison walls. However, when they finally surfaced, they found themselves crawling out of their tunnel *right beside a parked police car, with two officers in it!* Everyone was immediately recaptured, and Sutton was transferred to Holmesburg County Prison, which was supposed to be even more secured. That was a stroke of luck for Sutton. He escaped from Holmesburg in less than a month.

This time, Sutton was determined to stay out of trouble. He took a ferry to Staten Island in New York City's harbor and got a job as a janitor at The Farm Colony, a vast, rambling old folks' home for abandoned seniors.

During the seven years he managed to hide out at the Colony, Sutton really did make a serious effort to overcome his addiction to robbing banks. But to his surprise and chagrin, so many heisters were now copying his famous bank robbing method that he began being blamed for all kinds of robberies he hadn't committed. It was bizarre. Here he was, innocently pushing around a broom in an old folks' home, working hard to resist the temptation to even case a bank, while on the streets of New York City the police tally of bank robberies attributed to him grew like the score at a basketball game. On a few occasions, Sutton was even blamed for robbing different banks in different parts of the city at the very same time!

Finally he gave up. What was the point of trying to stay clean when everyone out there was convinced you were robbing more banks than ever before? Sutton moved back into the city and began to case another bank—the Manufacturer's Trust on 14th Street and 10th Avenue.

It was the last bank he would ever case.

On Monday, February 18, 1952, Sutton was riding on a subway train in lower Manhattan when a young man named Arnold Schuster began looking at him very thoughtfully. Sutton was busy thinking about his plans for the Manufacturer's Trust and failed to notice the young man following him when they both got off at the Pacific Street station. He didn't see Schuster hailing a police cruiser and pointing excitedly. He didn't realize he was in trouble until three officers drove up to the curb, surrounded him, and asked for identification.

It was the beginning of the end of Sutton's career as one of America's most famous bank robbers. The jury took one look at his astonishing criminal record and sentenced him to life in prison. He was sent to serve his time in New York State's awful, riot-prone Attica Prison.

Given his sentence, Sutton might well have died in prison. But he didn't. He escaped once more—but this time he applied his own bank robbing approach. He avoided digging, smashing, shooting, or brute force. He used ingenuity instead—and his opponent's unintended cooperation.

He did it by studying the law.

He studied it for 17 years before he finally found the answer. It was a technicality that allowed him to appeal his life sentence and have it reduced to the amount of time he had already served. Nobody believed he'd be able to win such an appeal, but with the help of several dedicated lawyers he did. He was released in 1969, at the age of 68.

Sutton never returned to bank robbing. By the time he was released from Attica, he was too sick, weak, and tired. He was also broke. (He never revealed what had happened to all that hidden loot.) During his final 11 years of life, he earned a modest living as a bank's security consultant, advising his former victims on how to avoid being robbed by people like himself. He even made a series of television commercials, promoting the credit cards of the New Britain Bank & Trust Company in Connecticut. (In the commercials, he held up his NBBTC credit card and said: "See? Now when I say I'm Willie Sutton, people believe me!") He also worked on his memoirs with journalist Quentin Reynolds.

Willie Sutton died a poor but free man in 1980. He was 79.

The Notorious Purolator Caper

ON SUNDAY, OCTOBER 20, 1974, at 6 o'clock in the evening, two vehicles traveling in convoy along Chicago's Congress Expressway took the Ohio Street exit and headed for the intersection of Huron and LaSalle. That was where the Chicago headquarters of the Purolator Security Company was located—a massive boxlike cement building that bristled with guns, alarms, and vaults full of cash.

The Purolator Security Company provided businesses all over North America with huge, well-guarded warehouses in which they could store their daily earnings or their excess cash. The company also provided armed pickup and delivery. Most businesses didn't like to keep too much money in their own safes at any one time.

The two vehicles, an Econoline van and a sedan, were driven by two cousins, Charlie and Tony Marzano. Charlie was a truck driver who also owned a suspiciously large amount of real estate. He specialized in burglar alarms—not installing them, but disconnecting them. Tony was also a trucker—and he specialized in bogus credit cards and airline tickets on the side.

The two men parked their vehicles a few blocks from the Purolator building and turned on their walkie-talkies. They waited anxiously for a signal.

They had been doing this every Sunday at 6:00 p.m. for three weeks now. And each Sunday, Ralphie had eventually radioed the same brief, disappointing message: "Forget it."

Today, after about 20 minutes, their sets finally came alive with a different response. "It's okay," they heard Ralphie say in a low voice.

Ralphie Marrera was a night watchman at Purolator. He was tall, dark, and easy-going—famous for telling jokes with punch lines that nobody could understand. Despite his modest guard's salary, Ralphie also owned an awful lot of real estate—a hotel, a gas station, a duplex, and other properties. Earlier that year, he and Charlie had been implicated in a million-dollar Chicago jewelry robbery, but not prosecuted for lack of enough evidence. Somehow this information had never come to the attention of the Purolator Security Company.

Tonight, Ralphie was on duty in Purolator's front lobby, watching a bank of television monitors. He had a walkie-talkie on the counter in front of him.

"Come on in," he spoke into the set.

Through his side window, Tony could see Charlie punch the air in an ecstatic victory salute and start up the van. Charlie headed directly for Purolator's big garage doors on Huron Street. Tony followed slowly in his sedan, scanning all parked and moving vehicles as he went. He stopped on the shoulder of LaSalle Street where he could see the van pulling up to the Purolator doors and keep an eye peeled for any outside trouble. "Unit One to Unit Two, I'm ready," he heard Charlie say.

Nothing happened for about five minutes. Tony could see Charlie through the van's side window, looking around nervously.

What was the hang-up now? They were sitting out here like ducks in somebody's rifle sights!

"*Open the damn door!*" Charlie's voice hissed.

Still no response from Ralphie.

Finally, the door slowly began to rise. As soon as it was high enough to clear the van's aerial, Charlie tromped on the gas and the van lurched inside. The door sank back down.

The radio silence for the next 15 minutes just about drove Tony crazy.

Even though Charlie had explained it to him a dozen times, Tony still expected the cops to come screaming around the corner or to burst out of the building any second. It just didn't seem possible that a huge score like this could be so simple.

Ordinarily, on a weekend, there would have been two other guards in the lobby with Ralphie, and a plan like Charlie's wouldn't have had a chance. But over the past several months, Ralphie had begun offering to cover for his fellow guards during their shifts on weekends. They could go home early, or take an extra couple of hours for supper, or catch a movie at a nearby theater. Both had happily agreed, because nothing ever happened on weekends. The whole place was shut down and nobody was around. You could lose your mind watching the motionless scenes on those boring security monitors hour after hour. So tonight, one guard was at the theater and the other home for an extended supper break. The place was wide open for at least three hours.

"Okay," Charlie's voice finally crackled through Tony's radio. "We're all set."

Throwing a last look around the intersection, Tony got out of his car, then hurried across the street and up to the garage door. He kicked it once, sharply. It hummed and rose. He ducked under and it closed again.

When his eyes adjusted to the gloom, Tony found himself in a vast, high-ceilinged maintenance garage. All around him, silent

Purolator armored vans stood parked in neat rows, or raised on jack-stands for repairs. The Econoline van stood just inside the door, its panel door pulled open. Charlie stood at the top of a nearby stairway, beckoning.

Even with all this excitement going down, Tony found himself thinking the same thing he always thought when he looked at Charlie: The guy dressed like a bum. Cheap red ski jacket, cut-rate pants and fake-leather loafers. It was amazing, really. Charlie owned millions of dollars' worth of real estate, but he still shopped at Buy-Rite Bargains, lived with his wife and kids in a modest bungalow in a rundown part of Chicago's Little Italy, and drove beater cars. You had to wonder what was the point in tackling the likes of Purolator if none of it was ever going to show.

Tony himself preferred rich-grain leather jackets, dress shirts, calfskin boots and, after his recent divorce, lots of female company. True, monthly child support and taking out the ladies was expensive, which was why he didn't own much real estate—actually, he didn't own *any* real estate—but at least he had something to look forward to most nights. And if they hit the jackpot on this score, he'd be able to buy himself a fancy townhouse on Rush Street and a membership in Faces, the classiest disco club in Chicago. It set you back $300 to join, but it was worth every nickel.

"You coming up anytime soon?" Charlie called from above.

Tony sprinted up the stairs, his footsteps echoing loudly against the high interior walls.

Charlie led the way through a dark corridor, the blaze of light from his powerful flashlight bobbing and weaving ahead of them. They passed through several gates and barriers, then up more stairs. Finally, they stopped at a massive steel door, so heavy that Charlie had to hand Tony his flashlight and use all his strength to open it. It led into a cavernous interior that looked to Tony like an enormous tomb.

"The vault room," Charlie explained.

Before them in the murk stood two massive freestanding vaults, looking like grim bomb shelters. The door to one of them had already been deactivated and opened. Charlie stepped inside. "In here," he said.

What Tony saw inside made him go weak in the knees.

Hundreds of canvas bags and metal footlockers filled with cash. Tons of it. Bags of cash stacked almost to the top of the high ceiling. Enough money, by the look of it, to buy half of Chicago.

"Jeez," he said. "We should have brought a moving van."

Charlie shrugged. "Yeah, probably," he agreed. He handed Tony a pair of surgical gloves. "Come on. Let's get started."

AN HOUR AND A HALF LATER, Tony sagged against the rear wheel of the Econoline. His face was red, his legs were shaking, and his shirt was soaked with sweat. He'd heard that people always underestimate the weight of money, and now he knew it was true. "I've had it," he told Charlie, who was dragging two more bags of cash into the van. "I really mean it. Get Ralphie down here to help."

Charlie wasn't looking much better. He had stripped to the waist, and his entire torso was wet with sweat. He had a long scratch across his stomach and his dripping hair was plastered across his forehead. "Just a couple more," he muttered hoarsely. "Come on, man; there's room for a couple more."

Tony groaned. "Those springs'll bust," he said.

"We're only driving a coupla miles," Charlie pointed out.

They staggered back up the stairs for a final load.

Back in the vault, Tony looked at the mountain of bags still untouched and sighed. An hour and a half of steady hauling, and they'd barely put a dent in all that money. It didn't look as if there was any missing at all.

It was a crying shame.

Suddenly, Ralphie's voice squawked from the walkie-talkie in the pocket of Charlie's shirt lying on the floor, making both men jump. "Another 20 minutes at the most," he warned. "Guy watching the movie's gonna be back soon."

Charlie shoved four more moneybags out into the corridor and then began to set out gasoline-filled plastic jugs. He positioned each jug in a nest of money-bags, then linked them all together with a long cotton wick. He attached the final length of wick to a timing device, set to explode just after midnight. The resulting fire would obliterate all traces of the theft, and when the police and firemen arrived, they'd be investigating a fire, not a break & entry.

Charlie checked the timing device one last time and closed the vault door. "Tell Ralphie we're on our way," he said.

THE POLICE AND THE FIREMEN who responded to the fire alarm at the Purolator Security Company on Huron and LaSalle at 1:12 a.m. on Monday, October 21, were met at the door by a shotgun-carrying Ralphie. He explained that company security regulations didn't allow him to let more than two people into the building at a time. He didn't know about any fire; his fire alarms hadn't gone off, but if the fire chief and the police chief wanted to come in and have a look around, he had no objections.

Since they couldn't see any obvious signs of a fire, the two chiefs agreed. They told their crews to take a break while they investigated.

The basement was fine, and so was the maintenance garage. They did, however, notice a faint haze of smoke over one of the vaults in the vault room.

They had to call Purolator's night supervisor out of bed to come open the locks.

When the supervisor pulled open the door, a dense black cloud of smoke swirled out of the vault, almost choking the three men.

"That's arson," the fire chief said.

They found the insides of the vault smoke-blackened and scorched in a few places, but otherwise unharmed. Eight plastic jugs full of gasoline were still sitting unburned in their nests of moneybags; two others had obviously burned for a few moments but then died. A melted timing device lay a short distance away.

"They build these vaults practically airtight," the fire chief said. "Not enough air in them to feed a fire. Not if you close the door, there isn't."

THE REPORTS IN TUESDAY'S NEWSPAPERS all over the US made the unidentified gang that had robbed the Purolator warehouse sound enormously sophisticated. Since there were no signs of a break-in, and no entry alarms had been triggered, and since nobody knew about Ralphie's involvement or the temporary absence of his fellow employees, it was assumed that the entire robbery had been cleverly conducted under the very noses of the three unsuspecting Purolator guards who had been on duty at the time—defeating some of the most technologically advanced alarm and sensor systems known to man. (Curiously, no one mentioned anything about the bungled arson attempt.) The $4.5 million haul was, to date, the biggest single theft of cash in American history—bigger even than the $2 million Brinks job in Boston in 1950, or the $1.5 million post office job in Plymouth in 1962. In fact, it was second only to the world-famous Great Train Robbery that had occurred in England in 1964.

The media's conclusion: Obviously, such a complex operation could only have been pulled off by the Mob or some international crime cartel—professionals who, by now, were undoubtedly already half a world away with their booty.

WELL—NOT REALLY. If the media or the public had known how the robbery had *really* been accomplished and just how "sophisticated" this gang *really* was, they might have been very disappointed. Or, more probably, they would have laughed their heads off.

Here's what happened during the next few days.

About half an hour after the robbery, Charlie pulled the heavily loaded Econoline into the garage of a friend who'd agreed to lend them his place for the night.

"You in all the way?" Tony called from behind. "Only a coupla more inches! Give it a try!" Charlie tried. The van surged forward, crashing into the garage's front wall. There was a loud splintering of boards and timbers, and the garage roof sagged down onto the van roof. They were in.

Dragging the bagfuls of money into the basement to count them made the two men so thirsty, they drank half a dozen celebratory beers. By the time they'd counted about half a million dollars, they were so parched they had to drink a lot more celebratory beers. By 3:00 a.m. they'd had to restart their count so many times they finally gave up.

At 3:30 a.m., somebody by the name of Frenchy arrived with an empty suitcase and left after Charlie had filled it with about $200,000. (Tony didn't recognize him, and Charlie didn't explain.) At 3:45 a.m., Tony and Charlie headed out in Tony's sedan to deposit Ralphie's share (about $2 million) in another garage. At 4:30 a.m., they stopped at a traffic island, and seconds later a car pulled up so close that their mirrors scraped. Charlie told Tony to hand across a suitcase containing about $100,000 (again, he didn't explain), and both vehicles screeched off in opposite directions. At 5:00 a.m., Tony and Charlie pulled into a Denny's Restaurant parking lot and shut off the motor.

There were only two other cars in the lot—both big black Lincoln Continentals. One contained a large, dangerous-looking man named Pete Gushi and his very grumpy wife, who was still dressed in curlers and a faded pink bathrobe. She was driving. Pete Gushi was the proprietor of a fencing operation disguised as a family discount store, and was rumored to be a Mob enforcer on the side.

The other black Lincoln belonged to Louie DiFonzo, a stockbroker who specialized in money laundering. Louie always wore cashmere sports jackets and fancy handmade leather shoes. He was so obsessed with his appearance that Tony had once claimed he spent "about six flippin' hours a day" combing his hair.

Charlie had asked DiFonzo and Gushi to avoid attracting attention by parking on opposite sides of the parking lot, but the two cars were parked side by side with their windows open, the two men yakking loudly. Both vehicles had their motors running.

THE PLAN WAS FOR A FINAL $400,000 payoff to be made in this parking lot at 5:30 a.m. (once again, Charlie wouldn't say to whom—this was driving Tony crazy). Then, Charlie, Tony, and Pete would take the remaining $1.8 million and head for Miami in Tony's sedan, with DiFonzo following in his Lincoln as the crash car. The crash car driver's job was to "accidentally" crash into any police roadblocks and divert the police while the others fled. Once they'd reached Miami, all four of them would ship out to Grand Cayman Island on a boat arranged by Pete Gushi. The Cayman Islands was a tiny three-island nation whose main attraction to crooks and tax evaders was its conveniently secretive banking laws, which allowed people with money they needed to hide to stash their loot in conveniently unidentifiable bank accounts.

Everyone waited—and waited. If any of the local precinct's police had shown up for their usual morning donuts, they'd have stumbled upon the entire crew, complete with almost $2 million in stolen cash, loaded shotguns, and walkie-talkies in their trunks. But that morning the police chose to have their donuts somewhere else.

By 6:00 a.m., their connection still hadn't shown up and Charlie was becoming nervous. He proposed that Gushi's wife should take home the $400,000 and hide it, while the rest of them carried on with the plan. Everyone agreed except Gushi's wife, who caused a tremendous ruckus, hollering that there was no blinking way she was going to drive home in a car full of stolen loot, with every cop in Chicago out looking for them! It took Gushi at least 15 minutes to calm her down.

After Gushi's wife finally agreed and everyone got ready to leave, DiFonzo discovered he'd locked his keys in his car—with his engine still running. They had to get a coat hanger from

Denny's to break into his car. It was almost 7:00 a.m. before Charlie's ragtag crew finally pulled out of the Denny's parking lot and headed south on Highway 90.

The trip—and the plan—began to crumble almost as soon as it had begun. DiFonzo drove so slowly that not only was he useless as a crash car, it wasn't long before they'd lost him completely. He didn't catch up with the rest of the gang until lunchtime, when he caught sight of Tony's car at a roadside restaurant.

Then Pete Gushi went off to make some phone calls about the boat to the Cayman Islands, and came back to announce that the arrangements for the boat had fallen through. (In fact, Pete Gushi had completely forgotten to make any arrangements for a boat.) That really irritated the rest of the gang, because arranging for the boat was really the only thing that Gushi was contributing to this caper. Charlie had to work hard to cool everybody down again.

So what to do? DiFonzo suggested they fly. He knew an outfit called Executive Jet Service that would fly you anywhere in a private jet. He looked them up in the phone book and discovered that Executive Jet had an office in Columbus, about two hours' drive farther southeast. "How much to fly four guys on a fishing trip to the Cayman Islands?" DiFonzo asked into the phone. "Forty-six hundred? Hey Charlie! Forty-six hundred bucks to fly us to the Caymans?" Every head in the restaurant turned in their direction.

Charlie sighed and nodded.

Once they'd been settled in their rented Lear jet for a while, high over North Carolina, the pilot mentioned customs clearance. How did they want to handle going through customs when they got to the Caymans?

Charlie almost choked on his rye and cola. Customs? Jeez, he hadn't even thought about customs. The main reason for using a boat to get to the Caymans had been to avoid customs altogether.

No chance of that, the pilot said. The way George Town Airport was laid out, there was no way you could avoid customs. But hey, what was the problem? There was no way Cayman Islands Customs was going to impound a bunch of fishing equipment!

But Charlie had been to the Caymans before, and he knew the Lear jet's flight crew would be going through customs at the same time as their passengers—and there was no way he wanted them to see what was in his duffle bags. "I'll tell you what," he told the pilot. "Change of plans. We've got some business in Miami that needs doing. Drop us off there." The pilot looked puzzled, but nodded.

At Miami International Airport, Charlie insisted everyone get into the same cab. All the duffle bags had to be squeezed into the trunk. The cabbie could barely get it closed. "Where to?" he asked. Charlie hadn't gotten around to thinking about that. "Make it...ah...make it The Colonnade," he said finally, because that was the only hotel that popped into his mind.

THAT TURNED OUT TO BE A BIG MISTAKE. The minute they arrived in the lobby of the Colonnade they sensed something was wrong. Terribly wrong. Everywhere they looked they recognized fellow crooks. And all the faces they *didn't* recognize sure looked like cops. The more they looked, the more they realized they *were* cops! Charlie turned quickly and began dragging his duffle bag back toward the front door.

"Let's get *outta here!*" he hissed at the others. They'd already come to the same conclusion. All four scrambled back out the door and flung their bags into the nearest cab. "Where to?" asked the cabbie, startled at having four men leap into his car as if they were being chased by a pack of bloodhounds. "*Anywhere!*" Charlie hissed. "*Anywhere! Just drive!!*"

They'd totally forgotten about "The Convention."

Each year in November, several thousand of America's most brazen hustlers and con men get together in Miami to spend a week partying their brains out in plain view of the police. This year, the hotel chosen for the event had been The Colonnade. So the Purolator heisters, who had just made headlines all over the country for the biggest vault robbery in American history, had walked straight into the biggest gathering of cops and robbers in the US, with almost $2 million worth of red-hot banknotes almost bursting out of their luggage!

Luckily, none of the policemen or FBI agents in the crowd recognized them.

THAT NIGHT, the four men celebrated their narrow escape in the bar of a cheap Miami motel, with a steady stream of drinks. The place was a dump and the band was terrible, but as time went on and the drinks multiplied, everything started looking better and better. It must have looked absolutely terrific by the time they called it a night, because when they woke up the next morning, they were presented with a $3,000 bar tab—*and* a $75,000 bill for the band! Apparently, they had bought it—the manager showed them the contract, laboriously written out on a table napkin and signed by Pete Gushi.

Charlie, of course, hit the roof—especially when he found out that Gushi had also phoned his wife the night before, despite Charlie's express orders that no one was to reveal their location to anyone back in Chicago. His mood wasn't helped much when Gushi reported that Ralphie had been arrested for complicity in the heist—and that Purolator's insurer, the Commercial Union Insurance Company, had posted a whopping $175,000 reward for information leading to a full recovery of the stolen money.

It was the largest such reward ever offered in American history.

At that point, Charlie decided to send Gushi back to Chicago—his drinking and his big mouth were becoming too much of a problem. The new plan called for DiFonzo to take the loot to Grand Cayman by regular commercial airliner—he was the only member of the gang without a criminal record—and Charlie and Tony would follow on a later flight. Charlie told DiFonzo to deposit the money temporarily in the Cayman National Bank and then check in at the George Town Holiday Inn and wait.

"Check in under the name of Frank Martin," he instructed.

But when Charlie and Tony arrived at the George Town Holiday Inn, there was no one by the name of Frank Martin registered at the hotel. The next day, they checked with the desk again. Still no Frank Martin.

"That sonofabitch has run off with our money!" Charlie fumed. "I'm calling Chicago—he won't get far."

Tony knew exactly what "calling Chicago" meant. The days on this earth for Louie DiFonzo were numbered.

They were just heading for the payphones when Tony spotted DiFonzo sitting nonchalantly under one of the lobby's palm trees, combing his hair. "Where the devil have you been?" Charlie demanded. "We've been looking all over for you."

"I was looking for you myself," DiFonzo said. "Why didn't you call my room?"

"We tried—but there was no Frank Martin registered."

"Oh damn," DiFonzo admitted. "I forgot about the Frank Martin part."

Down in the bar, he told them the amusing story of how he'd passed through Cayman Islands Customs. The six duffle bags were so heavy, he'd had to ask several passengers to help him lug them up to the counter. The customs agent had looked at the bags suspiciously.

"Any alcohol or contraband in these bags?"

"No, sir."

"Mind if I have a look?"

"Go ahead."

The agent had unzipped the first bag and dug around with his hands. No clothes, no personal possessions, no booze, no merchandise. Nothing but dozens of bundles of US banknotes.

"Okay. How about that bag? Any alcohol or contraband in that?"

"No, sir."

"Mind if I have a look?"

"Suit yourself."

The agent unzipped the second bag, then the third. He plowed his hands through the bundles of banknotes, up, down, around, but found no drugs, no alcohol, no contraband.

"Okay. What about all those?"

"Same thing. Just money."

The agent closed up the third bag. "Okay. Enjoy your stay. Next!"

All three men laughed uproariously. "The Cayman Islands," Tony chortled. "What a place to do business, huh?"

For the next three days, DiFonzo—whose job in this caper was to use his stockbroker's knowledge to invest the gang's money in profitable ways—earned his share of the loot by investing it in half a dozen Cayman Islands banks.

BACK IN CHICAGO, heads were rolling at the FBI's Illinois office.

Barely 14 hours after the Purolator robbery, the FBI discovered *it had already known about the heist!* In fact, it had known about it at least six weeks before it had even happened!

Dates, names, places—pretty much the whole story.

They'd gotten it all from a small-time fence named Larry Callahan, who'd been arrested for theft in the summer of 1974. In return for a suspended sentence, Callahan, who worked in Pete Gushi's discount store, agreed to become an informer.

As early as September 1974, Callahan had reported to the FBI that Pete Gushi, the two Marzano cousins, and Louie DiFonzo were planning a huge job. He reported the purchase of the Econoline van, fake license plates, fake ID, various guns, and the plans for a boat trip to the Caymans. He even reported a planned date for the robbery: September 29. The only person Callahan didn't know about was Ralphie Marrera at Purolator.

So the FBI had everything but the group's target, and that proved to be their undoing, because September 29 was the day when Charlie and Tony first pulled up to Purolator with the Econoline van, but Ralphie radioed "Forget it." (One of his fellow guards had decided to stay on duty.)

At first, the FBI brass had just shrugged—maybe the crooks had experienced a minor hitch in their plans. But when nothing happened on the following two weekends either, they decided they were wasting their time. They called off their agents, closed the file, and focused their attention on more immediate matters.

A week later, the biggest burglary in the history of the US caught them all with their pants down.

BUT NOW THE FBI went into high gear. Ralphie Marrera was arrested on October 28. Tony Marzano was caught two days later at Chicago's O'Hare Airport—he had come home early, suffering from a toothache. Charlie Marzano and Louie DiFonzo were nabbed on October 31 in the George Town airport, about to fly to Costa Rica. They were immediately extradited to the US on charges of theft and grand larceny.

The key to the FBI's case became Pete Gushi. When Gushi was arrested soon after he returned from Miami, the FBI promptly hit him with a long list of charges relating to his fencing operation. With the Purolator charges piled on top, he was facing 20 to 30 years in jail, with no parole.

Gushi buckled. In return for a minimal sentence and a new identity under the Witness Protection Program—plus no embarrassing questions about what his wife had done with that $400,000 from the Denny's parking lot—Gushi sang like a meadowlark and sent all his burglar buddies to prison.

Which left the small matter of the $2 million that the gang had invested in Grand Cayman banks.

If they had hopes of retrieving that money after their jail sentences had run out, the gang was once again badly mistaken. A year after their trials, the Attorney General of the Cayman Islands asked the banks to return the money to Purolator—and they did. That finally put a wrap on what Chicago newspapers had called one of the most sophisticated vault robberies in history.

Introduction

Cassie Chadwick: *Scoundrels & Scalawags*. New York: The Reader's Digest Assoc., 1968.

Jimenez Moreno: McCormick, Donald. *Taken for a Ride*. Blandford, UK: Harwood-Smart Books, 1976.

Soapy Smith: Collier, W.R. *The Reign of Soapy Smith*. New York: Doubleday, Doran & Co., 1935.

Joe Weil: Brannon, T. *"Yellow Kid" Weil: Con Man*. New York: Pyramid Books, 1957.

Billy Miner: MacPherson, M.A. *Outlaws of the Canadian West*. Edmonton: Lone Pine Publishing, 1999.

Ned Kelly: Brown, Max. *Australian Son: The Story of Ned Kelly*. Melbourne: Georgian House, 1956.

Charles-Hippolyte Delperch de la Bussière: Llewellyn, Sam. *Small Parts in History*. New York: Barnes & Noble, 1992.

On the Run with Mona Lisa

Esterow, Milton. *The Art Stealers*. New York: Macmillan, 1973.

McMullen, Roy. *Mona Lisa: The Picture and the Myth*. Boston: Houghton Mifflin, 1975.

Reit, Seymour. *The Day They Stole the Mona Lisa*. New York: Summit Books, 1981.

Blowing the Vault at Laguna Niguel

Rosberg, Robert. *Game of Thieves.* New York: Arno Press, 1980.

Steele, Sean. *Heists: Swindles, Stickups, and Robberies That Shocked the World.* New York: MetroBooks, 1995.

Take the Money and Fly

Gunther, Max. *D.B. Cooper: What Really Happened.* Chicago: Contemporary Books, 1985.

Himmelsbach, Ralph. *Norjak: The Investigation of D.B. Cooper.* West Linn, OR: Norjak Project, 1986.

Rhodes, Bernie. *D.B. Cooper: The Real McCoy.* Salt Lake City: Univ. of Utah Press, 1991.

Hitting "Big Daddy"

Scoundrels & Scalawags. New York: The Reader's Digest Assoc., 1968.

Fairfield, William. "The Thief and the $80,000 Bricks." *Argosy,* 1956.

The Napoleon of Crime

Macintyre, Ben. *The Napoleon of Crime.* New York: Delta Books, 1998.

www.crimelibrary.com/gangsters_outlaws/cops_others/worth/ 1.html?sect=13

Banknotes from Heaven

McClement, Fred. *Heist.* Toronto: Paperjacks, 1980.

"Loot From Larder Lake Bank Robbery Recovered." *The Northern News,* Kirkland Lake. July 21, 1949.

"Robbers of the Larder Lake Bank Sentenced." *The Northern News,* Kirkland Lake. August 4, 1949.

The Classiest Thief in Manhattan

Hickey, Neil. *The Gentleman Was a Thief.* New York: Holt, Rinehart and Winston, 1961.

The Great Train Robbery

Read, Piers Paul. *The Train Robbers.* Philadelphia: J.B. Lippincott, 1978.

Delano, Anthony. *Slip-up—Fleet Street, Scotland Yard and the Great Train Robbery.* New York: Fitzhenry & Whiteside, 2004.

The Many Faces of Willie Sutton

Sutton, Willie. *Where the Money Was: The Memoirs of a Bank Robber.* New York: Viking, 1976.

Reynolds, Quentin, and Willie Sutton. *I, Willie Sutton.* (reprinted) New York: Da Capo Press, 1993.

The Notorious Purolator Caper

Marzano, Tony (with Painter Powell). *The Big Steal.* Boston: Houghton Mifflin, 1980.

The Chicago Tribune, various articles from October 21 to November 29, 1974, and April 15 to April 18, 1975.

Index

About the Author

ANDREAS SCHROEDER was born in West Prussia (today a part of Poland) and emigrated to Canada when he was five years old. He grew up on a British Columbia farm, but loved to read books and eventually became a full-time freelance writer. He has written more than 20 books, including poetry, fiction, and nonfiction, and has earned many awards and prizes for his writing. *Thieves!* is his second book for young readers; his first, *Scams!*, won a Red Maple Award.

When he's not writing, Andreas enjoys racing motorcycles, parachuting, flying paragliders, and downhill skiing. For 12 years, he also reported on famous scams and hoaxes from around the world for a popular national radio program. He lives on the Sunshine Coast in British Columbia.